the beginner's guide to martial arts

the beginner's guide to martial arts

Ray Pawlett

Published by SILVERDALE BOOKS
An imprint of Bookmart Ltd
Registered number 2372865
Trading as Bookmart Ltd
Desford Road
Enderby
Leicester LE9 5AD

D&S Books
Cottage Meadow, Bocombe,
Parkham, Bideford
Devon, England
EX39 5PH

e-mail us at:-
enquiries.dspublishing@care4free.net

This edition printed 2002

ISBN 1-856056-27-4

Creative Director: Sarah King
Editor: Clare Howarth-Maden
Project editor: Judith Millidge
Photographer: Paul Forrester
Designer: Axis Design

Printed in Singapore

1 3 5 7 9 10 8 6 4 2

contents

introduction

what are martial arts?

If you ask people 'What are martial arts?', the majority may no doubt have some picture in their mind of either a 'Kung Fu' film or a video arcade game. Many imagine martial arts to be both loud and heroic, with plenty of arm waving and aggressive gestures.

This image, whilst being vastly commercial, has very little connection with the reality that inspires millions of people around the world diligently to train in their chosen martial arts' style.

Martial arts' styles can also be classified as 'systems'. That is to imply that there is an input, a process and an output involved. A suitable image for a martial arts' system would be 'the Cauldron', which is taken from the Chinese book of the *I-Ching*.

In this image, the ingredients of our cauldron are some of the many different aspects of martial arts. The cauldron itself is the martial artist and the fire represents the spirit of the martial artist.

When heat is applied to the cooking pot, a transformation occurs. The ingredients will cook together to provide a nourishing meal. Although the pot will look the same from the outside, changes will have happened inside.

The true martial artist will gather together the different elements of their style in a similar way. He or she will then apply their own spirit in order to 'cook up' the ingredients. After a period of time the martial artist will be 'cooked', and an inner transformation will have taken place. This is not to say that you cannot keep adding ingredients, but it is a good idea to let the ones that you have in your pot start to cook at first.

The difference between a true martial arts' style and a sophisticated way of beating somebody up is that the artist will be seeking this type of transformation. The transformations are an ongoing process. You cannot become 'overcooked'.

Martial arts' training involves co-operating with your partner, as well as self-defence.

hard and soft styles

In modern times, the phrases 'hard' and 'soft' have been paraphrased to describe martial arts. The general perception is that hard styles are very athletic and therefore only suitable for the young and fit, and that soft styles are slow and therefore primarily for older people who are concerned with relaxation and stress reduction.

This is a major oversimplification of the truth. In the East, the difference is not considered to be as clear-cut. A true martial artist will need to gain at least an instinctive feel for what the hard and soft styles are. They will also need to respect both systems of working.

Hard styles are also called 'external' styles. This is because importance is placed upon muscular strength. Strength training will therefore be a part of the training syllabus. The movements will generally be in straight and direct lines of force. Common examples of hard styles are Karate, Tae Kwon Do, some Kung Fu styles, Ju Jitsu, Judo and Thai boxing.

Soft styles are also called 'internal' styles. This is because there is an emphasis upon using energy (*Chi* or *Ki*). Energy training, such as Quigong, will therefore be part of the training syllabus. The movements will always be curved and never in straight lines. Examples of soft styles are Tai Chi, Pa Kua, Hsing-I, Wing Chun and Aikido.

The hard and soft styles can be compared to each other using the common yin/yang symbol. In the yin/yang symbol, opposites merge into each other and become a part of the same thing. This is also true of the hard and soft styles of martial arts on a large scale and a small scale.

High-speed techniques are common in hard styles, while slower techniques are common in soft styles.

why different styles?

The final goal of all martial arts is the same: the raising of spirit. A common analogy is that all styles are different pathways to the peak of the same mountain. Yet the mountain will be of infinite height, as any master will admit that no one can know everything.

If this is true, you may ask yourself what the reason is for having all of these different pathways, as this is sure to cause confusion. Even within a single style of martial art, there are usually many different ways of executing the style. For example, within the Karate style there are different versions, such as Shotokan, Koyokushinki and Wado Ru. It is said by many masters that simply choosing your correct pathway is half the effort towards climbing your individual mountain.

The different styles are not there to confuse and bewilder the beginner. The real reason for the manifold varieties of style is simple. We are all different as people, so the style that we will prefer as individuals will therefore be different by necessity.

Another interesting aspect of martial arts is that they have usually been influenced by the history, folklore and customs of the country of origin. This is how martial arts' knowledge can also give you an insight into foreign cultures. Although there are many similarities between the styles, it is interesting to note the often subtle cultural differences.

A loud shout, or Ki Hap, can momentarily stun an opponent.

choosing a style

How do you choose the correct martial arts' style for yourself? Once you have decided that you would like to try to learn a martial art, how do you stop yourself from choosing the wrong path? Especially with modern-day advertising, which tries to attract students to a school.

The answer is simple. Pick a style that you like the look of and give it a try. Part of martial arts' training is having the courage to act on your own instincts. If it looks good to you, try it. The most difficult step to make is the first one. Once you have tried, many of the mental barriers that you thought existed will simply dissolve. A commonly quoted phrase in martial arts is that 'A journey of ten thousand miles has to start with the first step'.

If you stay conscious of what you are doing and follow your own inner self (another martial arts' skill), then it will not matter if you chop and change through several styles. This simply means that you are still trying to find the style that suits you the most. This part of the learning may take quite some time, but there can be many valuable lessons to be gained from it.

When you have found the style that is yours, nothing can stop you from training. It will become an integral part of your lifestyle. Motivating yourself to train is no longer the issue. It is more likely that you will find difficulty with not training.

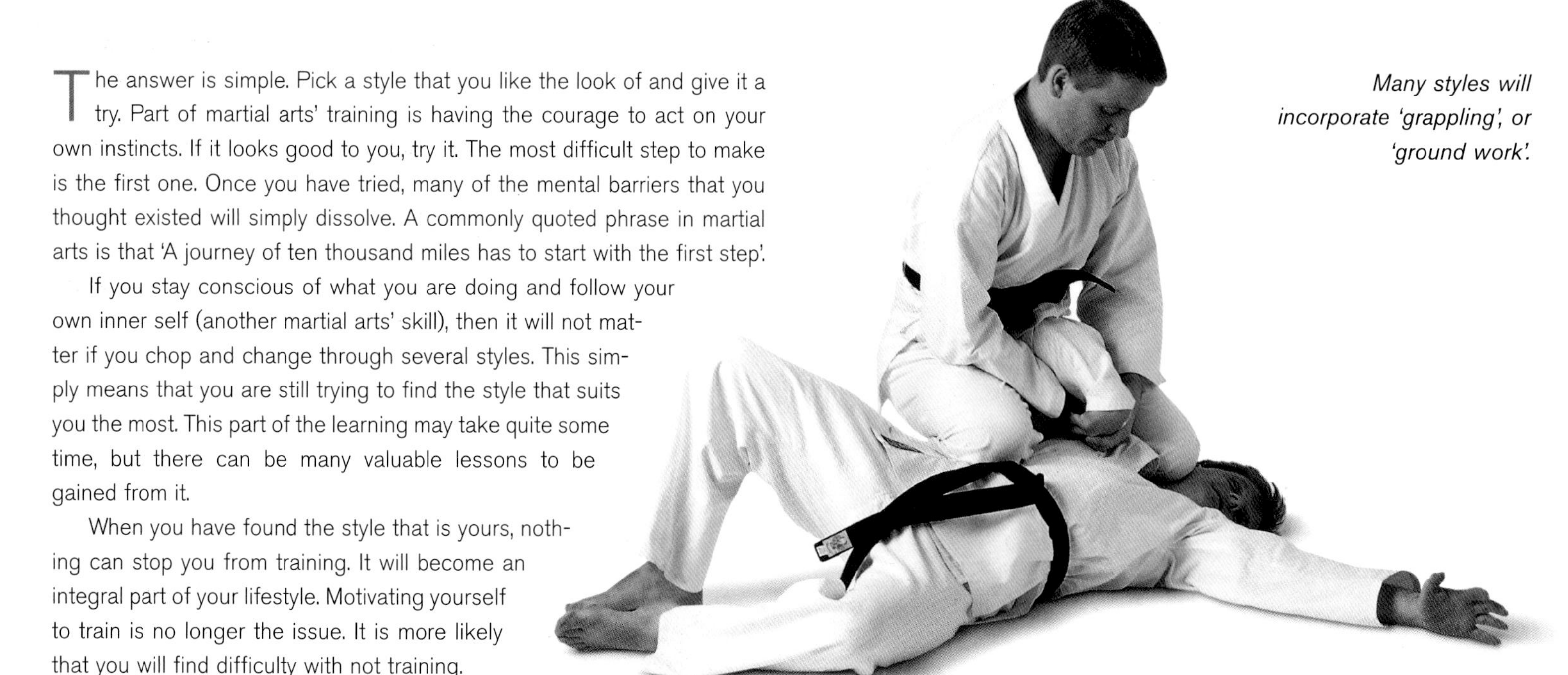

Many styles will incorporate 'grappling', or 'ground work'.

equipment

Most of the styles described in this book can be initially practised in T-shirts and jogging pants. When you have decided on the discipline that you wish to take up seriously, you will need to buy the appropriate suit or outfit.

Suits are similar in style, although a Judo suit will be of stronger material than a Karate-type suit, as many of the Judo sequences involve using your opponent's sleeves or lapels to throw them. For Tai Chi, you will only need a special outfit if you are entering a competition.

For disciplines that involve punching and kicking, you would be advised to purchase some protective gear, such as gumshields and groin boxes. Your instructor will advise you on the exact requirements.

A lightweight and strong outfit is required for styles involving flying kicks.

grading

Most of the disciplines in this book allow you to progress through a series of gradings. The details for each discipline are given in the relevant chapters. Whatever your choice, however, there are some important points to consider.

During a grading you will be asked to demonstrate your knowledge of a certain number of techniques that form part of your grading syllabus. When you can show competence in the required techniques, then you will be awarded with the grading.

Many beginners ask the question 'How long until I am a black belt?' The more experienced martial artist will understand that a black belt can only be gained through serious training – it does not simply depend on the amount of time that you have spent studying. It is useful to remember that it could be dangerous to wear a black belt if you are not up to it. The belt makes a statement that you have reached a certain skill level, and this will be assumed during training.

Anybody can go to the shop to buy a black belt. It is what you know about your style that defines you as being a true black belt. Gaining your black belt is only the start of another journey, during which you will have to gain an even deeper insight into your art.

warm-up exercises

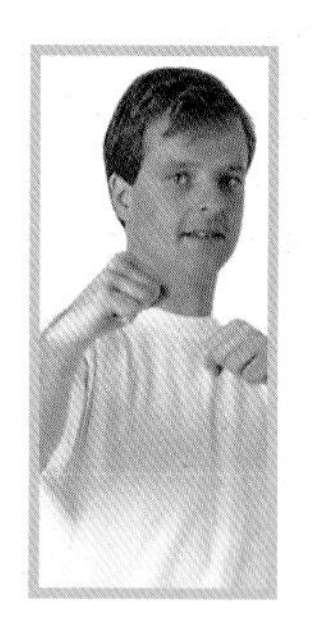

why warm up?

If you ever visit a sporting event, whether it be a martial arts' tournament or a football match, you are almost certain to witness the contestants warming up. If a competitor has reached the stage where they are entering events that will be seen by others, they will understand the importance of warming up.

The first and most important reason for warming up is safety. If you have practised a warm-up session and some stretches, your muscles will become more flexible. This will help you to avoid incurring strained muscles. If you are practising sparring, for example, warming up will give you the flexibility to move quickly without hurting yourself. Be careful never to strain your body. If an exercise is causing you pain, your body is giving you a message that you should stop. If you do not listen to that message you will be risking injury.

Another reason for warming up is that it prepares you mentally. It helps you to forget the other parts of your life and to concentrate your energies on your practice session. This is a vital ingredient towards success. If you cannot focus your attention, you become ungrounded and your movement will have no definition.

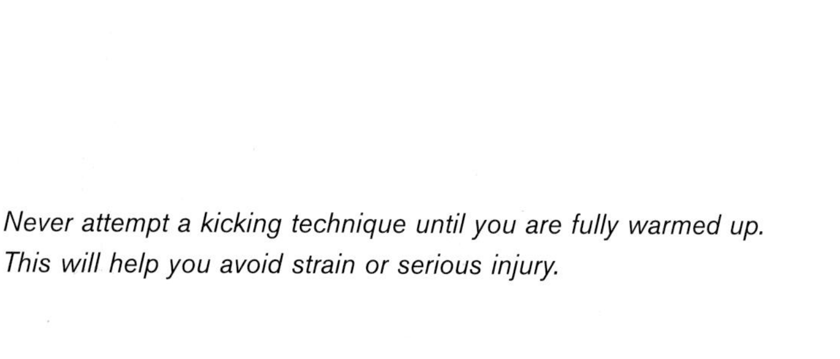

Never attempt a kicking technique until you are fully warmed up. This will help you avoid strain or serious injury.

warm-up routine

A typical warm-up routine will begin gently to mobilise the joints. As the pulse rate rises, the exercises become more cardiovascular. This will work the heart and lungs strongly. Finally, you will stretch to aid flexibility.

Exercise 1 ● neck rotations

Your neck is a vulnerable part of your body. A slight injury to your neck will stop you from training and can be painful. It is therefore important to loosen up your neck.

Start by standing firmly, with your feet approximately a shoulder width apart. Lift through the crown of your head, but do not strain. Look forwards.

Imagine that you are drawing a circle with your eyes. Make the circle increase in size by increasing the size of the rotation. Try to make the circle as big as you can without hurting yourself. (See steps 1 to 4.)

When you have loosened in one direction,, come back to the centre and reverse the direction.

1

2

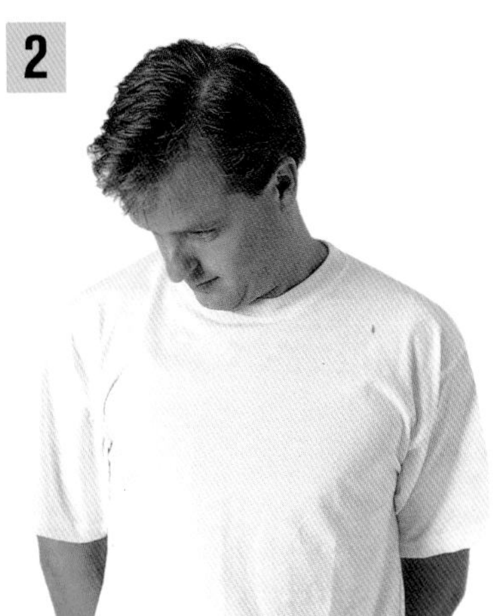

3

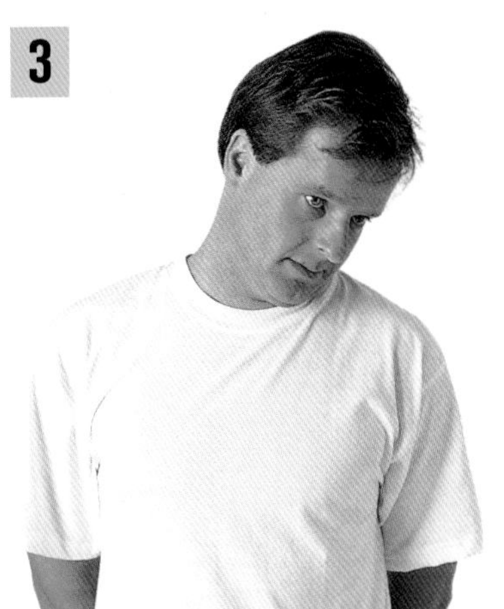

4

Exercise 2 ● shoulder rotations

Elements of modern living, such as driving and computer work, can cause tension in the shoulders. If an area is under tension it becomes stiff, then it becomes prone to injury.

Start by standing firmly, with your feet approximately a shoulder width apart. Lift through the crown of your head, but do not strain. Look forwards.

1 On your inward breath, raise your shoulders.

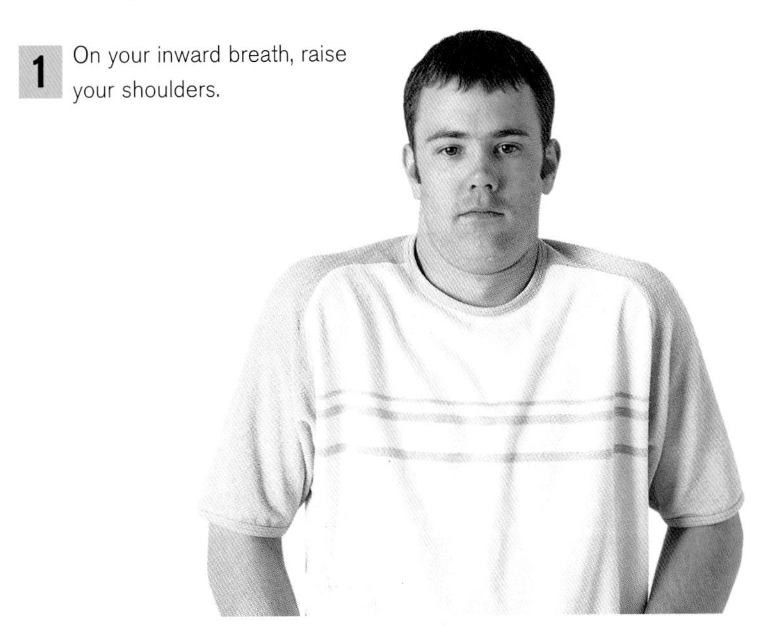

2 On your outward breath, lower your shoulders. Move your shoulders in a circular fashion and control the movement so that it co-ordinates with your breath.

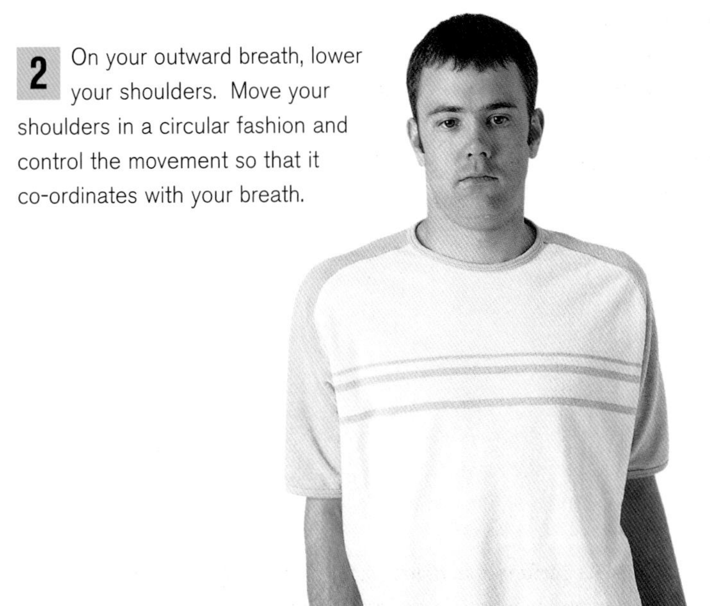

exercise 3 ● waist rotations

Back injuries are very common and debilitating. A large percentage of back injuries occur in the lower back area. The next two exercises teach you how to strengthen and loosen the lower back and the waist. This can help to protect you from lower back strain if you learn how to use your body correctly. Start by standing firmly, with your feet approximately a shoulder width apart. Lift through the crown of your head, but do not strain. Look forward.

1 Place the palms of your hands on your kidneys. Start by making small circles with your waist. Gradually increase the size of the circles in an outward spiral. You have reached the maximum circle size when it becomes difficult to keep your head in the same position.

2 After you have practised for some time near the maximum, come back to the centre in decreasing spirals until you come to a stop.

Repeat the exercise, moving in the other direction.

Exercise 4 ● swinging the waist

This exercise helps to loosen the waist and the top half of your body. Start by standing firmly, with your feet approximately a shoulder width apart. Lift through the crown of your head, but do not strain. Look forward.

1 Rotate your body clockwise and anticlockwise. Allow your arms to hang loose, so that they swing out under their own momentum. Do not simply swing your arms, but instead let your waist become the source of the movement.

2 Gradually increase the amplitude of the movement to increase the benefit of the exercise. Do not overdo the exercise by either swinging too hard or stopping suddenly, as this can cause injury.

Exercise 5 ● knee rotations

Knee injuries are very common in athletics and martial arts. The majority of knee injuries can be avoided if the knees are warmed up properly in the first place.

A simple, but effective, way of warming up and strengthening the knees is by knee rotations. As with any other exercise, you should not attempt it if it causes you discomfort or if you have a previous injury that may be worsened by the exercise.

Start by placing your feet together, with no gap between them. Place your hands on your knees to give them a little extra protection.

Begin to make small circles that gradually spiral outwards to form bigger circles. When you have done several in one direction, slow down and come back to the centre. Now repeat in the other direction

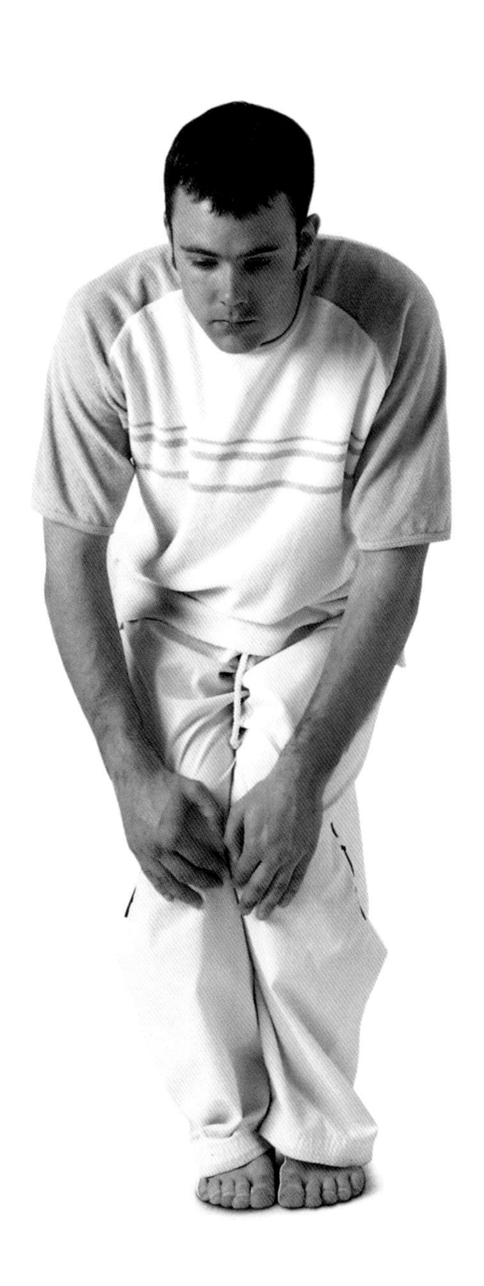

Exercise 6 ● ankle rotations

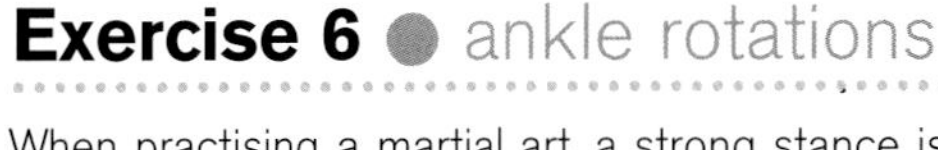

When practising a martial art, a strong stance is required, no matter what style you are studying. If your ankles are weak or tight, the whole of your posture is adversely affected. If you are practising a style that involves kicking, ankles become even more important, because they are being used in unfamiliar ways.

A simple ankle rotation will loosen the ankle and leg and aid the coordination of your feet.

Start by touching your big toe on the floor. Make circles with your knee, so that the ankle joint is worked in a circular pattern. When you have made several rotations, reverse the direction and then change to the other leg.

Exercise 7 ● rotating the knee

This exercise loosens the hip joint and strengthens the leg muscles.

1 Start by lifting your knee as high as you can in front of you.

2 Now draw an outwardly moving circle with your knee. Repeat the exercise several times and then change direction. Repeat for the other leg. This exercise can be done at any speed. It becomes more difficult (and works better) if you slow it down.

Exercise 8 ● leg raises

Leg-raising benefits co-ordination and balance, as well as being a vigorous warm-up exercise.

1 Stand in a strong stance, such as a bow or front stance.

2 Push your weight down on to your leading or front leg and raise the other as high as you can. Keep your leg straight, but do not lock the knee. The objective of the exercise is to loosen up your hip joint and leg. It is therefore more important to keep your back straight during the exercise than to try to get your foot as high as you can. Give yourself some time and you will be able to lift your foot high without hurting yourself.

When you have performed 10 to 15 leg raises on one side, repeat on the other side.

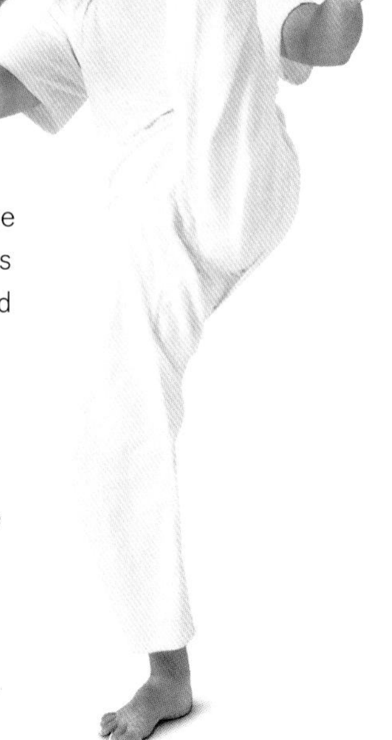

Exercise 9 • reach and jump

The next two exercises are designed to work your heart and lungs. Use your knowledge of how your body works to build up the amount of repetitions that you do. There is little point in performing too many repeats of these exercises if your energy is then spent for your training session!

Start by bending your knees and going into a crouched position. Take an inward breath. On the outward breath, jump as high as you can and try to reach up for the ceiling. You will soon find that your breath will naturally co-ordinate with your movement.

When you land, come down with the balls of your feet before the heels and try to absorb the impact. If you land on your heels it can send a shockwave through your spine, which can be injurious.

Exercise 10 • spin and jump

This exercise teaches you how to move from your centre. When you have mastered how to control your movement from your waist, the exercise becomes easy.

1 Begin the exercise by taking up a standing stance.

2 Jump up and try to spin your body through a full circle. If you gain sufficient height and spin from your waist, you will soon find that you can master the exercise.

Repeat by spinning in the other direction.

Exercise 11 ● leg stretches

Strong and supple legs are a requirement of all martial arts' styles. There are three important things to remember when stretching:

1. you must be **WARMED UP**
2. stretch **SLOWLY**
3. if it hurts, **STOP.**

If you ignore any of these, you will risk injury.

Butterfly stretch

Sit on the floor, with your knees bent and the soles of your feet together. Try to bring your knees as close to the floor as possible. Never force your knees down. Allow your body to dictate how far it will stretch.

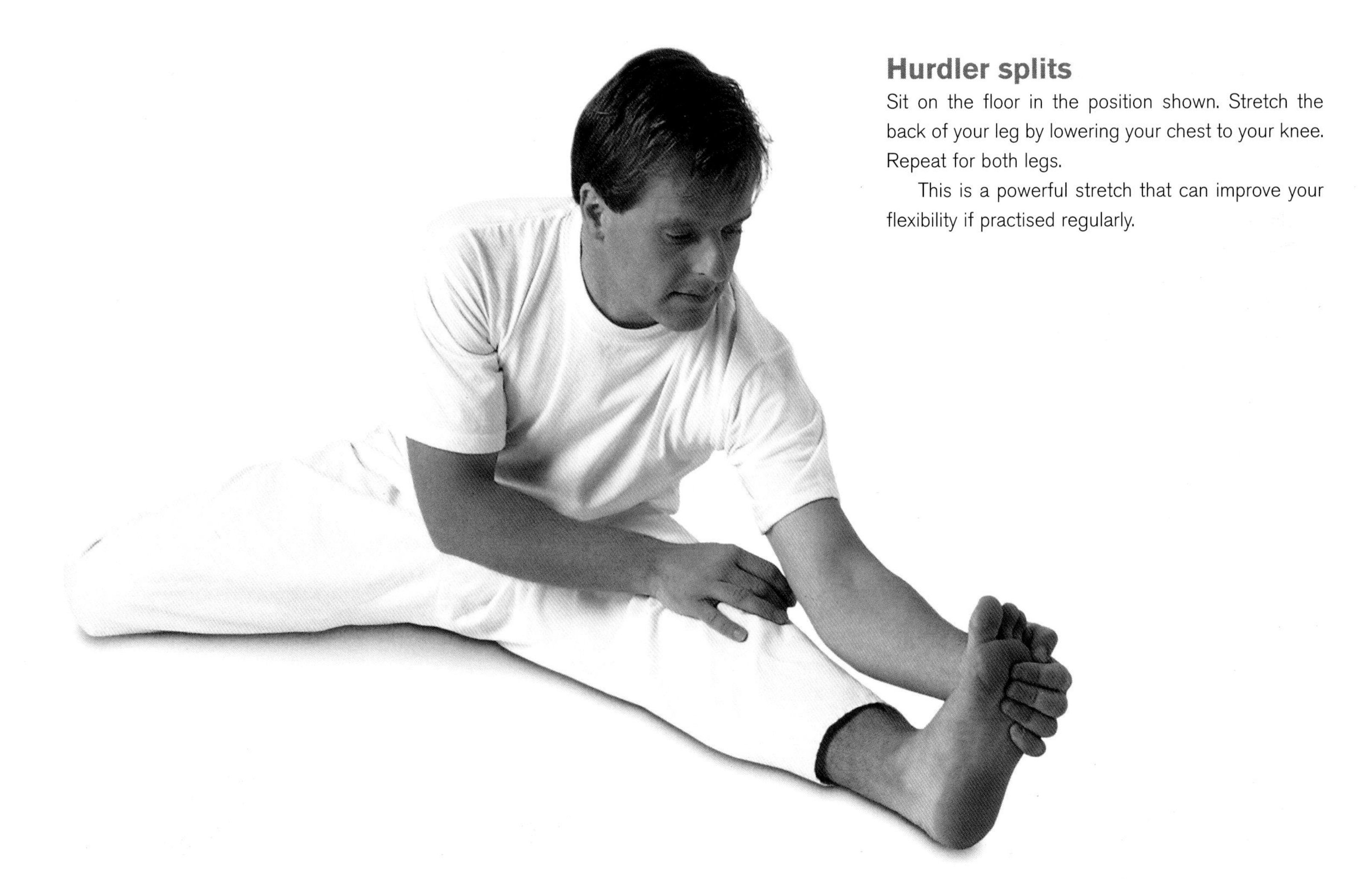

Hurdler splits

Sit on the floor in the position shown. Stretch the back of your leg by lowering your chest to your knee. Repeat for both legs.

This is a powerful stretch that can improve your flexibility if practised regularly.

karate

what is karate?

Karate should more accurately be called 'Karate Do'. 'Do'' means 'way' and 'Karate' means 'empty hand'. The translation of Karate Do, then, is 'the way of the empty hand'. When we talk of 'empty hand', we mean that unarmed combat is assumed. It is true that some styles will teach students how to use weapons, but the spirit is within the empty-hand forms.

Karate tends to concentrate more on developing powerful punches and kicks than on locking techniques and throws. This is the main difference between it and Judo or Ju Jitsu. That is not to say that there are no locking techniques or throws within the Karate systems. There is an overlap between some of the styles, but the difference in emphasis should be understood.

The 'way' of Karate is to learn responsibility for your skill. There is always a great emphasis upon respect for one's self and for others within the Karate Dojo (hall). On the memorial to Gichin Funakoshi, the 'father' of modern Karate, there is the statement, 'There is no first attack in Karate'. This statement helps you to understand the 'way' in the terms that the father of Karate saw it.

The sporting side of Karate has become very popular in recent years.

history of karate

The roots of Karate lie in the Okinawan Islands, just off Japan. They were originally an independent state, but came under China's power in 1372. In 1429, the carrying of weapons was banned. This led to the vigorous study of empty-hand systems, so that the people could defend themselves.

In 1772, an Okinawan named Sakugawa coined the phrase *'karate-no-sakagawa'*, and the style was given its name for the first time.

In 1922, Gichin Funakoshi introduced Karate to Japan. He demonstrated Karate very successfully. It was not, however until he met Jigero Kano, the founder of Judo, that his own philosophy and teachings developed in a way that would make Karate a recognised martial art.

By 1936, Karate had become widespread, and Funakoshi had his own purpose-built dojo constructed. Funakoshi also had the pen name Shoto, which literally means 'pine waves'. 'Kan' is the Japanese for hall, so the name given to this dojo soon became Shotokan, and the name of the style practised there was given the same name. The Shotokan style of Karate had been born.

Other styles such as Kyokushinkai, Shukukai and Wado Ryu also began to develop in parallel with Shotokan. The different styles may place emphasis in different places, but they are still all recognisable as being Karate.

After the war, Funakoshi undertook a tour of the USA in 1952 at the age of 84. By doing this he ensured that the seeds were sown for Karate to develop in the West. He died in 1957, aged 89, and, unlike his contemporary, Jigero Kano, was able to see his lifetime's work spread around the world to be practised by millions.

Karate teaches you how to deliver high-impact techniques to vulnerable areas of your opponent's body.

Striking techniques may also be used as blocks. This strike is more famously known as the 'Karate chop'. Note it uses the edge of the hand – not the fingers.

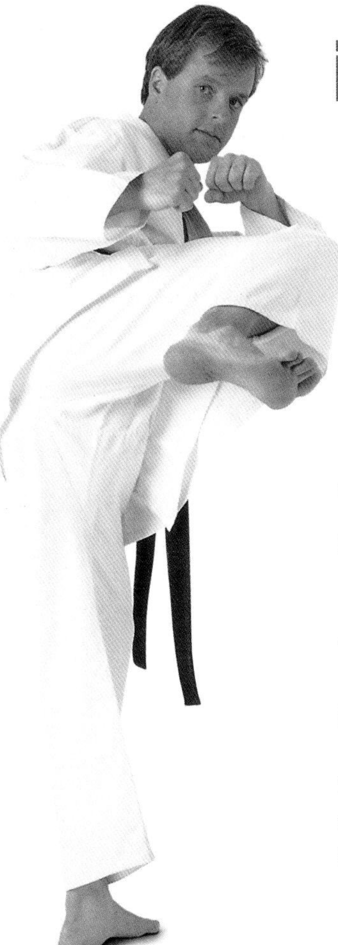

is karate for me, and what do I need?

Karate is both mentally and physically demanding. No matter what your level of fitness, you will eventually encounter something that will make you work hard. The same can be said of most martial arts' systems. If you are willing to make changes to your lifestyle if it is an unhealthy one, then there is no reason why you should not be able to start to learn Karate.

There are two types of injury associated with this style of martial art. The first is the type of injury that is caused by overuse or strain. This is entirely avoidable if you warm up thoroughly, follow your instructor's advice and know your own limits.

The second type involves the knocks and bruises that you can gain during any contact sport. You will find that the number of these injuries is far less than you may expect. The reason for this is that any sparring is done under carefully controlled conditions. It is true that accidents will happen, but if you compare martial arts to any other contact sport, such as football or rugby, in this respect, then you will probably be less put off.

grading

The focus of grading in Karate is around the kata. To gain your white belt, you should be able to perform the Kihon kata and understand the movements. As you progress though to black belt, the kata will become longer and more demanding. You will also be asked to show your kumite (sparring) basics and your understanding of Karate Do. When you perform your kata, the grading instructor must be able to see that you understand the meaning of the movements according to the level that you are currently at. The complexity of the meanings increases as you rise through the gradings.

As an example, what is seen as a block to a white-belt kata may also be seen as a strike or throw to a black belt.

The grading pattern is as follows

Novice	White belt
9th Kyu	Orange
8th Kyu	Red
7th Kyu	Yellow
6th Kyu	Green
5th Kyu	Purple
4th Kyu	Purple and white
3rd Kyu	Brown
2nd Kyu	Brown with white stripe
1st Kyu	Brown with two white stripes
1st Dan	Black

karate exercises

Karate involves many explosive movements, such as punches and kicks. Some Karate styles also use a long and low stance. It is therefore vital that you loosen your ligaments and joints if you wish to avoid injury. Warm-up exercises should stretch and strengthen your muscles.

Windmill the arms

This exercise loosens the arms and shoulders, improves co-ordination and works your cardiovascular system.

2 Rotate the arm.

3 Repeat on other arm.

1 Start by throwing one of your arms over your shoulder in a circular fashion.

You can use combinations of both arms in the same direction or spin your arms in different directions. If you find the exercise difficult at first, stop thinking about it and it will soon become easier.

Press-ups

The traditional way for press-ups to be done in both Karate and Tae Kwon Do is on your knuckles. This helps to condition your knuckles for your punching practice.

1 Start in the basic press-up position, remembering to keep your back straight.

2 Allow your body to come close to the floor. Keep that back straight!

3 Push up to the starting position and repeat several times.

Forward bend

This exercise is ideal for loosening your hamstrings and spine.

1 Start with your feet a shoulder width apart and look forward.

2 Bend from your waist and keep your back straight.

3 Allow your body to drop down. If you cannot grab your ankles or feet, then grab your Gi to stabilise you. Be sure to bend from your waist and also to keep your knees straight.

If you wish to make the exercise more difficult, then bring your feet closer together.

Side stretch

This exercise will help you to loosen through the sides of your body.

1 Start with your feet a shoulder width apart and look in front of you. Lift your right arm and place your left hand by the side of your left leg.

2 Pull down with your left hand and over with your right. You will feel the right side of your body stretching.

Repeat for the left side.

dachi - stances

A good stance provides the stability from which you can execute your technique. It follows that if you do not have a good stance, then good technique will be impossible. In most Karate styles, such as Shotokan, long and deep stances are employed.

This is to give you the maximum stability and develops very strong legs. If you wish to improve your Karate, stances are a good place to start. In the following examples, the demonstrators have gone into the stance from a feet-together position. This is only for clarity, as there are many different ways of adopting the stances. Your instructor will teach you the other starting postures if you decide to proceed.

Zenkutsu dachi ● front stance

In this stance, the majority of your weight (60 to 70 per cent) is on your front leg. This gives you a powerful driving force for a forward attack.

2 Keep your weight on your left leg and slide your right foot forward. If you can keep your balance properly, you will be able to execute the movement in a smooth and controlled way.

Push your right foot forward as far as you can to go into the full stance. The power for the push should come from your back leg.

3 Keep your feet flat on the floor and a shoulder width apart. The angle of your back foot should be about 45°.

1 Start with your feet together and your knees bent. Place your hands on your hips and look forward.

Kokutsu dachi ● back stance

The weight distribution for back stance is the reverse of that for the front stance, that is, 60 to 70 per cent of your weight is on your back leg. It is useful when you may need to move backwards out of a situation.

1 Assume the same starting position as for the front stance, with both of your feet together and your hands on your hips. Move your left foot straight forward. Keep the left knee bent and your weight on your right leg.

2 Rotate your waist to slide your left foot further forward. Keep both knees bent.

Kiba dachi ● horse-riding stance

Kiba dachi is called the horse-riding stance because it looks like the student (Karateka) is astride a horse. The weight distribution is equal, so the stance will work from the left- or the righthand side. When you have strengthened your leg muscles, you will find that it is a very solid stance.

Kiba dachi is a simple stance that you can move straight into by placing your feet two hips width apart, with your toes turned in slightly and your knees turned out.

uke - blocks

Blocks are probably the next most important thing after stance in your Karate training. There is little point in being able to deliver the most devastating punch if you cannot stop your opponent from attacking you. A well-placed block is able to open an approach for your next attack.

Gedan barai ● downward block

This block is used to protect your lower area, that is, your groin and legs.

1 Begin in the starting position used for the stances.

2 Hold your left arm in front of you and bring your right fist near to your left shoulder.

3 Keep your upper body still as you move forward with your left leg, ready for a front stance. Thrust your right foot into the front stance. Simultaneously block down with your right hand and pull back with your left.

Application

This block could be used to block a front kick to your groin.

Age uke ● rising block

This block is used to defend an attack to your face or head.

1 Start from our standard feet-together position. Bring your arms forward, ready to move into a front stance. Move your right foot forward.

2 Thrust yourself into the front stance. Simultaneously execute the upper block with your right arm and pull your left fist back to your waist.

Application

This block can be used to deflect a punch to your face.

uchi waza - strikes

In Karate, when we talk about strikes we normally refer to open-handed strikes or elbow strikes rather than kicks or punches. Various parts of your body can be used to strike at a weak part of your opponent's body. Some strikes lend themselves to an attack on a certain area better than others.

Do not be tempted to 'test' your strikes on roof tiles or by breaking boards until your instructor thinks that you are ready. It may sound ridiculous, but this is a common cause of broken bones!

To perform a strike, there is always a preparation movement and a striking movement. Both are illustrated here, together with an application for each strike.

Knife hand strike

This is an extremely powerful strike. It is known around the world as the 'Karate chop'. It uses the fleshy part of your hand, between the little finger and your wrist.

Application

This strike would be very dangerous if used to attack the neck.

Preparation

Extend your left hand and raise your right hand to your ear. Rotate your body away from the target slightly.

Strike

Simultaneously rotate your body, retract your left hand and strike. The power comes from using the whole of your body, so it is crucial to time the retraction of your left hand and the strike with each other.

Nukite ● spear finger thrust

This attack uses the extended fingers to gain penetration. It is therefore only useful for soft areas of the body, where it is very dangerous. Pull the tip of your middle finger back, so that the striking area is formed from the three extended fingers.

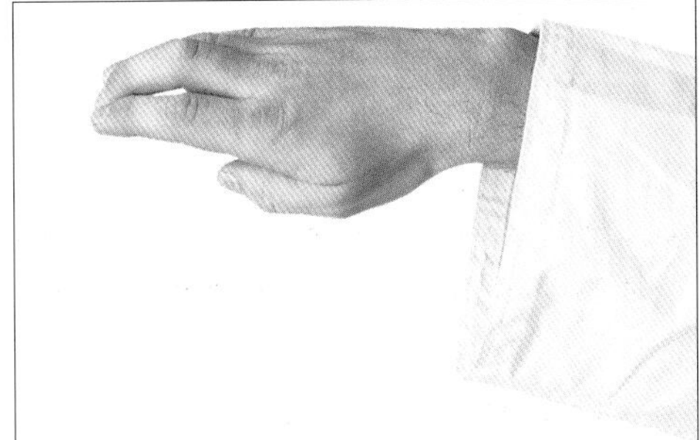

Preparation

Extend your left hand forward and bring your right fist to your waist. Turn your body away from your opponent's slightly.

Strike

Rotate your body, retract your left hand and strike with your right hand, all at the same time.

Application

A typical area for this strike would be the throat.

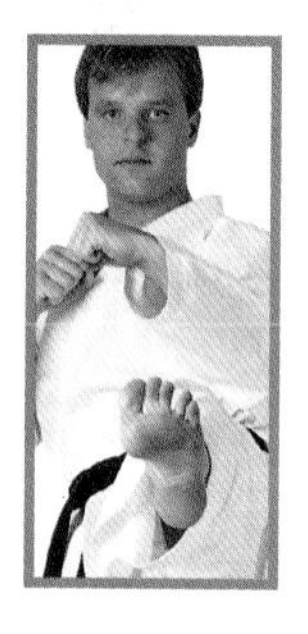

keri waza - kicks

Your legs are longer and stronger than your arms. If you can learn to kick without overbalancing, your legs will be formidable weapons. Striking with your feet is just as precise as striking with your hands. You need to know which part of the foot you are using and where you are going to place it.

Mae geri ● front kick

For a front kick, you should straighten your instep and kick with the ball of your foot.

1 Start from front stance.

2 Lift your right knee as high as you can.

3 Snap the kick forward using the ball of your foot.

4 Bend your knee immediately after performing the kick.

5 Settle back down to the front stance, this time with your left leg leading.

Application

The middle-section front kick is ideal for reaching through a person's range in order to strike at their abdomen.

Yoko geri kekomi • side-thrusting kick

If you are ever asked to break anything with a kick, then try to use this one. It is a very powerful kick and is ideal for breaking boards and roof tiles at demonstrations! Use the outside edge of your foot.

1 Start in fighting stance.

2 Lift your right knee and turn your waist.

3 Push your foot out, using your waist rotation and knee, to perform the kick.

Retract your foot to position 2. You could now place it on the floor or perform another kick.

Application

A typical target for a side kick would be the gap between the ribcage and pelvis.

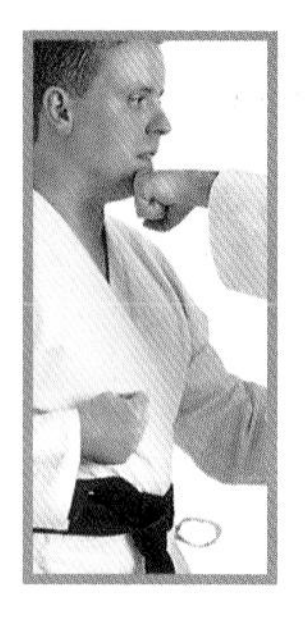

kumite - sparring

Kumite, or sparring, is a popular aspect of Karate training. Free sparring can be a good spectator sport and will test the Karateka to their limits. Karate is, however, a very controlled style. No Karateka should ever enter into the tournament arena until they are both physically and emotionally trained for it.

There are several stages that the Karateka will have to pass through before they are allowed on to the mats at a tournament. The different styles of Kumite, or controlled sparring, will help you to prepare for it.

Kihon ippon Kumite ● one-step sparring

In this type of sparring there will be a declared attack and counterattack. It is designed to help you to time your blocking and counterattack techniques with another person.

Example 1

A high punch is deflected and countered with a middle-section punch.

1 The attacking punch is deflected with a rising block.

2 A counterattack with a punch to the solar plexus.

Example 2

A front snap kick is deflected and countered with a high punch.

1 Step sideways and execute a lower block to avoid the kick.

2 Counterattack with a punch to the chin.

jiyu kumite – sports or freestyle Sparring

Freestyle sparring is not exactly what the name implies. There are some rules that are designed to protect both participants. Examples of these are that you should not strike at the throat or groin. Different associations will have different rules for their sparring.

An example is that in some styles, once you have scored a point, the fight will stop. In other styles the fight will be continuous and will not stop until the time is finished. The fight will normally be in two rounds that are two to four minutes long, with a short break in the middle.

Some examples of freestyle sparring are shown. You will note that the combatants are wearing foot and hand pads, which can be useful protection.

kata - the essence of Karate

One of the most important aspects of Karate training is pattern, or Kata, training. The Katas are designed to teach you the movements of the style that you are learning in a clear and succinct way. Imagine that every block or punch that you execute is against an imaginary opponent.

If you train this way, then you will be able to train with your Karate on 'full power'. Even in the most competitive free-sparring tournaments, you should not actually want to cause serious damage to your opponent. In Kata this is different. Your opponent is imaginary, so you should imagine that the spear finger thrust that you just executed has hit your opponent squarely on the Adam's apple.

This is how the difference between Karate as a martial art and Karate as a sport is defined.

The pattern shown here is the Kihon Kata. It is designed to teach beginners and is one of many Karate Katas.

Kihon Kata

1 Assume the starting position.

2 Turn left into the front stance and do a lower block.

3 Step forward, leading with the right leg, and punch.

4 Execute a 180° turn to perform a lower block in the opposite direction.

5 Step forward with the left foot and punch with your left hand.

6 Turn 90° to your original direction and execute a lower block on your left side.

7 Step forward and punch on the right side.

8 Step forward and punch on the left side.

9 Step forward and punch on the right side. Shout 'KIAI'.

10 Step behind with the right leg. Prepare to make a lower block.

11 Execute a lower block on the left side. Keep right hand close to body.

12 Step forward with your right leg and punch with your right hand.

13 Step behind with the left leg and prepare for a lower block.

14 Twist 180° and execute a lower block with the right arm.

15 Follow through with a punch from your left side. Keep right hand close to body.

16 Step to the left and prepare for a lower block. Execute a lower block with the left (you will be facing the opposite way from how you started).

17 Follow through with a punch from the right side.

18 Repeat with a punch from the left. Keep right hand close to body.

19 Punch again from the right side, while shouting 'KIAI'.

20 Step behind with your left leg and prepare for a lower block.

21 Execute the lower block with the left. Keep right hand close to body.

22 Follow through with a right punch. Keep left hand close to body.

23 Turn 180° and execute a lower block with the right arm.

24 Follow this through with a punch from the left side.

25 Return to the start position.

judo

what is judo?

Judo is the means of understanding how to make the most effective use of both physical and spiritual power and strength. By devoted practice and rigid discipline, in an effort to obtain perfection in attacking and defending, it refines the body and soul and helps instil a spiritual essence into every part of one's being. In this way it is possible to perfect oneself and contribute something worthwhile to the world.

(Jiguro Kano)

The wording of Jiguro Kano's definition of Judo may seem slightly dated, but the essence of what he was saying remains the same. He was explaining the differences between Judo and common grappling skills by the emphasis upon 'spiritual' development and contributing 'something worthwhile to the world'. These concepts should never leave the martial artist. It is what prevents the martial artist from simply being a skilled fighter.

Judo is called the 'Gentle Art'. Do not be deceived by this. It is a very practical fighting skill that will need both strength and stamina to learn. The gentle part of the art is more concerned with how you treat people off the mat than on it.

A properly executed Judo technique will allow a small person to throw a larger one.

history of judo

The origins of Judo have been fairly well documented. Unlike many of the older styles, such as Ju Jitsu and Kung Fu, we can actually name a person as being the founder of Judo.

Judo has its roots in Ju Jitsu. During the late 19th century, Ju Jitsu experts were using their skills in ways that were bringing the martial art into disrepute.

Dr Jigaro Kano was a Tokyo schoolmaster of the time. He had studied in various Ju Jitsu schools and wanted to combine the best of its skills into a physical activity that would challenge the minds of his students and teach self-discipline and respect for others.

He called this new system Judo, which literally means the 'Gentle Way'. There was an emphasis upon maximum efficiency, and the striking blows from Ju Jitsu were only taught to advanced students who were seen to have absorbed more of the moral codes. Many consider that by doing this, Kano managed to save the whole of the world of martial arts from falling into disrepute.

Kano had a very high respect for women. He taught Judo to women and undertook medical research with the experts of the time to prove that there was no reason why women should not practise Judo.

He also came to Europe in 1889 to teach the philosophy and practice of Judo. He died at sea in 1938, returning from the Cairo International Olympic Conference. There has been speculation that the enemies he made by teaching women and Westerners had him assassinated.

Since his death, Judo has become one of the most popular martial arts. It is an Olympic event that is practised by millions. The techniques have also been taught to police forces and soldiers around the world. If Dr Kano were alive today to see how his new and controversial style has benefited the bodies and minds of people around the world, he would be rightly proud of his achievement.

Above *From a standing position, the Judoka will use throwing techniques.*

Left *When on the mat, the Judoka will try to restrain their opponent.*

is judo for me, and what do I need?

The popularity of Judo is partly because it appeals to such a wide audience. It is suitable for all ages and you do not have to be any more fit than your neighbour to start learning Judo. You will find that continued practice will increase your strength, stamina and suppleness. This is a testament to the quality of the training rather than how fit you were in the first place.

Judo will involve some 'rough and tumble'. This is a quality that has made it popular for children. It can be a way to teach them how to use their natural energy in a constructive manner. If you suffer from brittle bones, you should take advice before starting Judo, as you will almost certainly take a few hard falls.

Judo is excellent if you enjoy being competitive. If you progress far enough, you will find many tournaments of regional, national and Olympic levels. If you are not the competitive type, you can still enjoy Judo. The difference is that you may not wish to enter the same tournaments as your more competitive classmates.

grading

When you have reached a level between intermediate and advanced, you will be taught Judo patterns (kata). Judo kata are different from most other styles because you perform them with a partner. This shows you how to harmonise with your partner, as well as teaching you the essences of the style.

The sequence of gradings for adults, from white to black belt, is as follows

9th Kyu	Yellow
7th–8th Kyu	Orange
5th–6th Kyu	Green
3rd–4th Kyu	Blue
1st–2nd Kyu	Brown
1st–5th Dan	Black

Juniors have a different grading system, where there are intermediate grades between the coloured belts.

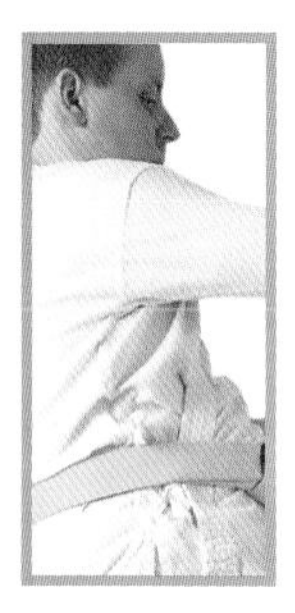

competition

One of the aims of Jiguro Kano was to develop a martial sport from Ju Jitsu. The wide range of Judo tournaments that are held in modern times bears witness to the extent of his vision when he invented the style.

If you enter a competition, you will be segregated by weight and sex. There is an open category in some events, but you will normally be at a disadvantage here if you are the smallest competitor.

All of the fights will be held on the mat and will be strictly controlled by referees and corner judges. The bout will last for a fixed time, depending on the competition that you are in. Points will be scored in various bands, and the winner is the contestant with the most points. If there is a tie, then the referee will have the deciding vote. The decision of the referee is final.

Points can be scored in the following ways: Ippon, Waza ari, Yuko and Koka, all of which are described below.

Ippon

Ippon is the maximum score. When Ippon has been scored, the contest will end. Ippon can be scored by completing a perfect throw, holding your opponent to the mat for 30 seconds or gaining a submission.

Waza ari

Waza ari is awarded for a near-perfect throw or for holding your opponent to the mat for more than 25, but less than 30, seconds. The scoring of two waza ari is known as waza ari awasete ippon and ends the contest.

Yuko

A Yuko is scored when the throw is not quite a Waza ari or if the hold lasts for more than 20, but less than 25, seconds.

Koka

Koka is called when an imperfect throw has been executed and the fighter has landed on his thigh or buttocks.

As you can imagine, there is room for doubt between the different types of score. This is where sportsmanship must prevail. Points will also be deducted or disqualification may occur for misconduct or foul moves.

etiquette

The spirit of Judo should be one of mutual respect for your fellow Judoka (students). This is demonstrated by the Judo players' etiquette to their fellows. Etiquette includes personal hygiene and the condition of your nails. It would be dangerous to have sharp nails.

Along with these considerations, you will need to learn the rituals involved around bowing, or Rei. Before the bout starts, you should bow to your judges. This is partly in acknowledgment of the fact that they are there for your benefit and not for their own.

Standing bow

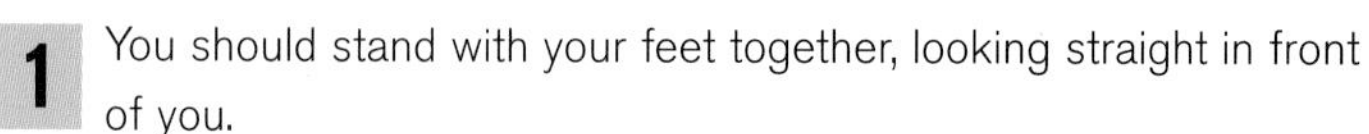

1 You should stand with your feet together, looking straight in front of you.

2 Bend approximately 30° from your waist. Your arms should be relaxed and your eyes should look straight at the floor.

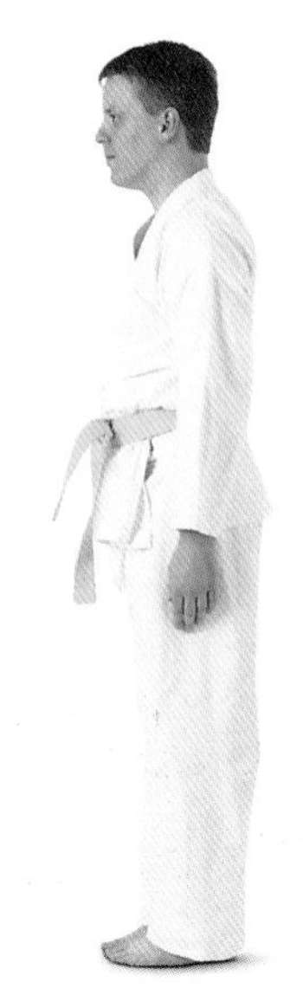

3 Before you start your bout, you should bow to your opponent as a sign of mutual respect. The bow is performed in the same way.

4 Make sure that you stand far enough apart. It is very embarrassing to have a head clash at this point.

judo exercises

Judo is a good way of keeping fit. You will need good stamina if you enter any competitions. The bouts may not seem very long to the spectator, but certainly seem long enough to the competitor. Any exercise that increases your stamina, such as swimming or running, will assist your Judo practice.

The following stretches are also useful, as you will need a strong and supple back to do Judo.

Cobra stretch

This exercise is borrowed from Yoga. Be careful not to overdo the exercise at first. Breathe evenly and let your body stretch naturally with the movement.

Back bend

1 Lie flat on the floor with your knees raised. Keep your shoulders flat on the floor.

2 Press down with your feet so that your torso lifts from the floor. Keep your shoulders flat on the floor.

Sit-ups

Strong abdominal muscles are important for Judo.

1 The easiest and best method is to practice sit-ups with a partner holding your feet.

2 Do not put your hands behind your head as this can cause neck injury. Instead, place your hands to the side of your head.

Uchi Kome

This is an important, two-person warm-up that practises the basic throwing moves.

1 Face your partner and take hold of their left lapel with your left hand. Your partner will hold your left sleeve with their right hand.

2 Step through with your right foot and bring your right arm under your partner's right arm.

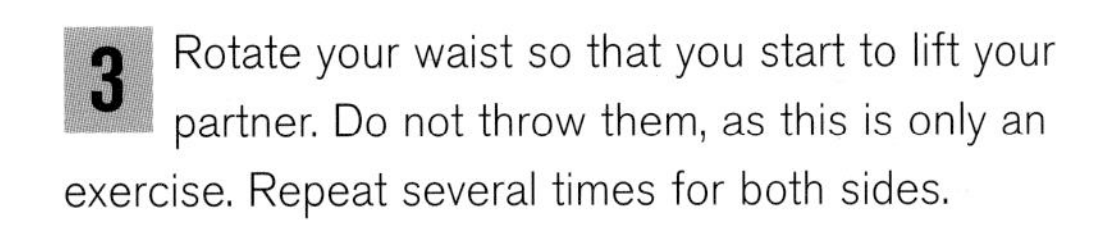

3 Rotate your waist so that you start to lift your partner. Do not throw them, as this is only an exercise. Repeat several times for both sides.

Break falls

Many Judo classes will begin with a round of break falls on the mat. Break falls are very important. When you practise Judo, you will be thrown. If you do not know how to land properly, you will be hurt. If your teacher incorporates break falls into your warm-up routine, then they will become easy for you.

Do not forget that if you are thrown you will not have time to think about how you perform a break fall. You need to practise them to such a level that they become instinctive. Once you have learnt to fall properly you will do so instinctively. This will be useful for avoiding serious injury in any circumstance – not just in judo!

Yoko Kaiteri Ukemi ● Sideways break fall

1 Bend your left knee and throw yourself forward, with your left arm outstretched.

2 Turn over completely. Make sure you continue moving. Do not stop at this point.

3 Upon landing, hit the floor with your right forearm to absorb the impact.

Ground break fall

Not all break falls are executed from throws.

1 This example shows how a break fall can be used to escape from your opponent's hold.

2 The arm that is not being held is used to break the fall and is ready for a countermove.

judo techniques

To the uninitiated, Judo can appear to be throwing and grappling on the mat, with no apparent technique behind it. This opinion would soon change if they ever tried a lesson. Judo is made up of a vast array of very clear and defined techniques.

A good Judo match is more akin to a strategic game of chess than just rolling around on a mat. If you realise that your opponent is trying to use a certain technique, you should use a countertechnique to beat them. This sounds easy enough, until you remember that your opponent will also be thinking about your strategy.

Simply speaking, Judo techniques can be split into standing work and ground work. The ideal, if you are standing, is to gain Ippon with the perfect throw. If you do not gain Ippon from your throw, you will need to try to restrain your partner or to gain a submission from your ground work.

The following is a selection of basic Judo techniques.

O Soto Gari ● outer reaping throw

This is a fairly simple technique that will be taught to you early in your Judo lessons. If a throw is a reaping throw, it means that you use your body weight to throw your opponent over your leg.

1 Grasp hold of your opponent's lapels.

2 Move slightly to the side of your opponent and place your right leg around the back of their right knee.

3 Twist your waist, so that your body weight shifts to your left leg, and pull down on your opponent's right arm.

4 Send your opponent to the floor by driving with your right arm, which should be holding your opponent's lapel firmly.

Ko Soto Gari • minor outer reaping throw

In this technique, you will sweep your left sole across your opponent's left heel to unbalance them. You will also need to unbalance your opponent with your hands.

1 Grasp hold of your opponent's lapels. You should stand firm, but relaxed.

2 Drag your opponent towards you and sweep the heel of their foot forward with the sole of your foot.

3 Complete the movement by pushing your opponent over your foot and unbalancing them. He cannot help but fall.

O-Goshi ● hip throw

This is an important basic throw that will form the foundation of more advanced throws. The secret is to get under your opponent's centre of gravity.

1 Grasp hold of your opponent's lapels. You should stand firm, but relaxed.

2 Turn into your opponent's chest. Push your shoulder firmly against him.

3 Wrap your arms around your opponent's back and push them over your hip.

4 Pull on your opponent's arm as you lean forward. This will unbalance him.

5 Complete the throw by rolling your opponent over your hip. Ippon!

Ko Uchi Gari ● sweeps

This is a simple, but effective, technique that has put many advanced opponents on the mat by taking them unawares.

1 Grab hold of your opponent firmly. Hook their foot upwards with a sweep from the sole of your foot. Do not kick their leg as this will incur a penalty point and the technique will not work properly.

2 As soon as you feel your opponent shift their weight, push forward with all of your strength so that you topple them.

Juji jime ● strangle hold

Juji jime is the collective name given to strangle holds. Here is an example of one called Kata juji jime, or the half-cross strangle.

1 Grab your opponent's right lapel with your right hand and slide it to the highest position that you can.

2 Grab your opponent's left lapel with your left hand, fairly close to the neck.

3 Rotate your wrists towards your opponent's throat. Be careful not to be overzealous with this technique, as you will already have won the bout if they have let you get them into this position!

Waki Gatame • armpit hold

This is another simple technique that will gain an instant submission if your opponent lets you get away with it.

1 You need to force your opponent face down on the mat.

2 Lean your back against your opponent's ribs and take hold of their arm. You will soon gain submission by pushing down on their upper arm with your armpit and levering their forearm upwards. This will render him immobile.

Kesa Gatame • scarf hold

This is probably the most popular form of hold-down technique.

Place yourself between your opponent's arm and body. Wrap your arm around your opponent's neck and press down with your body. You will need to spread your legs to stabilise your position and also to stay close to your opponent.

Ushiro Kesa Gatame ● shoulder hold

This hold is nearly impossible to escape from, as both arms are immobilised.

1 Start by taking a seated position alongside your opponent's head. Lie across their chest and spread your legs wide for stability.

2 Pass your right hand under their right shoulder. Control their left arm by gripping their wrist under your armpit and holding their sleeve firmly.

Ude Gatame ● armlock

This technique is the same as a rising block in Karate.

1 Your opponent reaches for you, which you deflect with a rising block.

2 Raise your other arm to their inner forearm.

3 Take control of your opponent by rotating their elbow joint.

tae kwon do

what is tae kwon do?

Tae Kwon Do is the most famous of the Korean martial arts. It is characterised by high kicks and energetic movements. There is more to Tae Kwon Do than just high kicks, however. Tae Kwon Do students will also learn powerful hand and joint-locking techniques.

Learning Tae Kwon Do will make your body very fit and supple. The stretching and stamina training in Tae Kwon Do can be extremely rigorous, and you will soon notice a big difference in your body, even if you have only trained for a few months.

Tae Kwon Do also contains a strict code of discipline. The Tae Kwon Do student will have to learn the responsibility of being a martial artist. This martial art also has a spiritual aspect that has its roots in Chinese Taoism and the *I-Ching*.

Traning and co-ordination is required to be able to perform jumping kicks to this high standard.

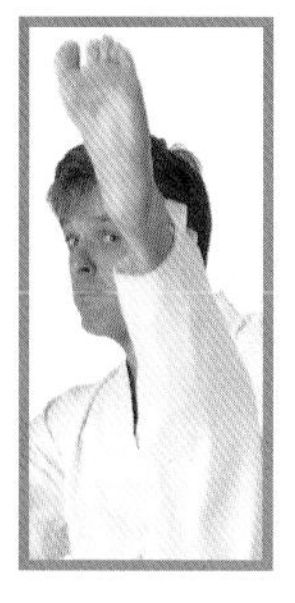

history of tae kwon do

The history of Tae Kwon Do is linked with the history of its native country – Korea. The history of Korea is complicated to say the least. Throughout history, Korea has tried to remain an independent state, although its geographical position was always going to make that difficult.

Korea has been subjected to many different cultures. It has managed to absorb the influence of these cultures, yet still retain its own identity. Tae Kwon Do is an example of this. The style was undoubtedly influenced by the Japanese, but it still remains a style of its own that is easily recognisable worldwide.

Tae Kwon Do (the 'way of hand and fist') has records that go back as far as 57BC. In 1935 three royal tombs for the Muyong-chong and the Kakchu-chong were excavated. These contained mural paintings that depict a style of martial art that looks very similar to the Tae Kwon Do practised today.

In AD 425 there was an official acceptance of Buddhism. This was to play a major role in the code of the Hwarang Do. The Hwarang Do were a warrior order with a tradition similar to the Arthurian legends of Great Britain and Europe. Their main task was to repel Japanese pirates.

Under King Taejo, the state religion shifted from Buddhism to Confucianism during the 14th century. One of the effects of this was that the martial art Subak, as it was then called, began to be practised by ordinary people.

The Japanese invasion of Korea in 1910 led to a complete ban on all martial arts' practice. Although the public practice of Tae Kwon Do was impossible, it was practised for the next 35 years by underground organisations such as the Independence Army and the Liberation Army. After liberation by the Allied forces in 1945, the practice of Korean martial arts was once more allowed.

Since then, many associations for Tae Kwon Do and other Korean martial arts have been formed. Most notably, the Tae Kwon Do style has become a style that is today practised worldwide, from community halls to Hollywood films.

In 1988 Tae Kwon Do was introduced as an exhibition sport in the Olympic Games held in Seoul, South Korea. It retained this status for the Olympic Games in Barcelona, Spain, but has been accepted as a full medal sport for the year-2000 Olympic Games in Sydney, Australia.

This axe kick is one of the many powerful kicks in the Tae Kwon Do style.

tenets of tae kwon do

Tae Kwon Do uses a strict moral code of practice that has been developed over the centuries by the Tae Kwon Do masters and monks studying the art. It is essential that anyone practicing Tae Kwon Do adheres to these tenets. They are a fundamental part of this martial art.

When asked in an interview what he looked for in his students, Master Park Jung Tae, who is one of the world's foremost authorities on the art of Tae Kwon Do, gave the following response:

1. courtesy
2. integrity
3. perseverance (through hard techniques and training)
4. self-control
5. indomitable spirit.

These are the 'Tenets of Tae Kwon Do'. These tenets are the crystallisation of many centuries of the study of the Korean martial arts. The same formula could easily be applied to any of the martial arts.

The wording of the tenets is deliberately simple, and yet also far-reaching. It starts with a basic requirement for the human condition. Think how different life would be if people showed genuine courtesy to one another. Indeed, many problems that we are experiencing in the world would simply disappear.

This reverse turning kick is a very fast and powerful technique.

is tae kwon do for me, and what do I need?

Tae Kwon Do is a fast and dynamic martial art. It will improve your suppleness and cardiovascular fitness. Many of the moves are quite athletic, and you will need to be reasonably fit before you can achieve a similar level to that shown here. As with all martial arts, it is especially important that you warm up well before beginning practice.

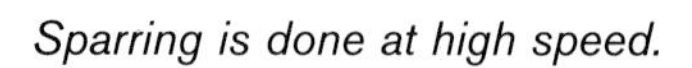

Sparring is done at high speed.

This gives you a clue about what the training will be like. Cardiovascular fitness and suppleness will not just happen overnight. You must be determined to succeed and work your body hard. In a Tae Kwon Do lesson you will sweat!

Free sparring is a feature of Tae Kwon Do. This may look dangerous, but is surprisingly free of injury if the exponents are disciplined. A groin box and gum shield will be vital if you start sparring properly.

Free sparring between experienced Tae Kwon Do students is an impressive sight.

tae kwon do exercises

If you want to learn how to make the spectacular kicks that are used in Tae Kwon Do, you will need to become supple. There are no shortcuts to achieving this. It will only come through regular training and practice. A supple body is less prone to injury than a stiff one.

It is an aspect of fitness that is frequently overlooked by many physical-education teachers. If you already excel in one sport, do not be shocked if you cannot stretch as easily as a trained martial artist. The trained martial artist will have spent a lot of time practising their stretching routines.

Stretches

When starting with your stretching, it is important that you are thoroughly warmed up. This will make your muscles softer and less likely to be damaged. Remember at all times that you can injure yourself through overstretching. Be very slow and careful. Listen to the messages that your body is telling you. Just because you can stretch to a certain point on one day, you may not be able to do it the next. Be careful.

If you are stretching in pairs, as in this section, you need to be sensitive to your partner's body. Listen to what they tell you. Even more importantly, try to imagine how they are feeling with the stretch. If you can understand your partner, you take a step closer to understanding your own stretches.

The following is a selection of assisted stretches that are used in Tae Kwon Do and other martial arts.

Axe-kick stretch

This stretch will loosen your hamstring muscles and will make the axe kick easier. Start with your back against a wall and lift up your leg. Your partner will then raise your leg slowly to stretch your hamstring muscles. Keep your toes back, so that your heel is forward. It is also important that you keep your back straight. Do not slouch and keep your standing leg firm, but relaxed.

Side-kick stretch

This stretch will work your adductor and abductor muscles. It is done in the position that you would be in for a side kick, but will improve your overall leg strength. Start with the side of your body against a wall and execute a middle-section side kick. Do not retract the kick. Your partner will then raise your leg to its maximum height. Keep your heel higher than your toes.

Floor stretch

This exercise will work with the abductor and adductor muscles. It will also stretch your torso.

For this exercise, you will both sit on the floor facing each other. The person who is to be stretched will open their legs. Your partner will place their feet on the inside of your legs and will gently push your feet.

Side-hip stretch

This exercise opens up the hip joint. It is a fairly basic stretch that can be practised by most beginners.

Remember to stretch both sides. Point your toes up to achieve the maximum stretch.

Front-split stretch

This is a more advanced stretch. In the beginning, you will not be able to stretch this far. Your muscles will gradually be trained so that you are able to do the splits. Do not strain your body – allow it to tell you how far it will go.

Box splits

This is the most difficult version of the splits. Some people can just drop into the splits on their first lesson. The rest of us will have to train long and hard to be able to stretch this far, however. Again do not force your body into this position.

punches

As Tae Kwon Do is well known for its powerful kicking techniques, it is sometimes presumed that this is at the cost of punching techniques. This would be a very dangerous assumption if ever you were to enter a tournament with an experienced Tae Kwon Do martial artist.

Many of the punching techniques in Tae Kwon Do have the same configuration as Karate punches. For the purpose of all except the most advanced students, these Tae Kwon Do punches can also be considered Karate punches.

The following is a sample from the range of punching techniques.

Forward punch

This is the standard martial arts' punch.

Back fist

This is a technique that pivots from the elbow rather than thrusts from the elbow. It is banned from tournaments as it is used on vital areas of the head. This makes it too dangerous to use unless you are in a genuine self-defence situation.

Reverse punch

This is similar to the forward punch, except that if your right leg is forward, then your left fist will be forward and vice versa. It is a very powerful punch and is frequently used for breaking techniques.

Hammer fist

This technique is similar to the back fist because it uses a pivot from the elbow. It is also banned from tournaments. It is popular in some Ju Jitsu lessons.

Upset punch

This is a surprisingly powerful technique that can be used at close range. It is frequently overlooked, because you have to remember that the fist is inverted, but it can sometimes help you to score the winning point in a difficult tournament.

Crescent punch

This punch is popular with boxers. The fist sweeps around in a circular path to strike the side of your opponent's head. The other hand is kept in close to your body. This is an effective punch if aimed correctly.

tae kwon do kicks

Tae Kwon Do is famous for its expertise in kicking. The kicks have both an aesthetic value and are very powerful. Along with the physical attributes of training, you will also need to develop a good sense of balance. You will need to remain calm and centred to practice these moves successfully.

The following is a selection of the kicks used in Tae Kwon Do. Remember that you should always seek training from a professional, as otherwise you could injure yourself when attempting these high kicks.

Turning kick

2 Rotate your hips and lift your knee until it has reached its highest position.

1 Start from any stance. Remember to keep your guard up.

3 Extend the kick. You could use your instep or the ball of your foot to strike with.

Back kick

1 Stand facing your opponent. Notice that the opponents in this picture are looking directly at each other.

2 Twist your body to face away from your opponent and lift your knee. Prepare yourself for making the kick.

3 Drive your heel into your opponent, underneath their guard.

Jumping back kick

This is the more advanced version of the back kick. Jumping allows you to aim for a different target and makes you more unpredictable. However, combining jumping and kicking requires plenty of practice.

Jumping front kick

1 Jump to gain height and close in on your opponent. You should prepare for where you will place your kick.

2 Your timing needs to be accurate to enable you to extend the kick at the correct moment.

Axe kick

The axe kick is used to smash your way through your opponent's guard and to hit them with your heel. Whatever it lacks in subtlety it makes up for in effectiveness.

Crescent kick

1 This is shown as a basic training technique, so the person kicking will not need to have their guard up.

2 Use the crescent kick to clear your opponent's guard and to open the way for a full attack.

fixed-step sparring

Fixed-step sparring is employed in Tae Kwon Do to sharpen your understanding of the techniques. There are different versions of fixed-step sparring. The one- and three-step versions are shown here. Three-step sparring is taught at beginner to intermediate grades.

All of the steps are pre-defined with an attack and a counterattack for the defender. When you progress to one-step sparring, you will frequently be asked to use 'any foot retaliation' or 'any hand retaliation'. This helps your instructor to assess how well you understand the suitability of the moves in different situations.

The participants will make each other aware that they are ready to start by calling 'Ki-Hap' to each other. Once Ki-Hap has been called, you need to be completely focused on what you are doing, as the attacker will be aiming punches that will hit you unless you block them.

The following are examples of one-step and three-step sparring.

Three-step sparring

1 Both opponents start by assuming the ready stance.

2 The attacker moves to the front stance, low-section block. The defender remains in the ready position.

3 The attacker punches with their right fist. The defender blocks the middle section.

4 The attacker punches with their left fist. The defender blocks the middle section.

5 The attacker punches with the right fist. The defender blocks the middle section.

6 The defender retaliates with a right reverse punch.

One-step sparring

1a The attacker punches their opponent.

1b The defender retaliates with a lower and upper turning kick.

2a The attacker punches.

2b The defender retaliates with an axe kick.

3a The attacker punches.

3b The defender retaliates with a reverse turning kick.

4a The attacker punches.

4b The defender retaliates with a side kick.

free sparring in tae kwon do

Tae Kwon Do is one of the few martial arts that uses full-contact, continuous free sparring. This type of sparring is strictly controlled. The only target areas are the front of your torso and your head. No strikes are allowed to the back of the head. A point will be awarded for a 'stunning blow'. This means, for example, that if you execute a perfect technique it will not gain you a point unless it hits its target properly.

Here are two Tae Kwon Do experts showing a sample of the techniques used in a tournament.

The opponents look for a chance to attack.

Sweeping past the face with a reverse hooking kick.

Counterattacking with a jumping back kick.

Attacking again with a turning kick.

Retaliating with a front snap kick.

Trying a turning kick with the other leg.

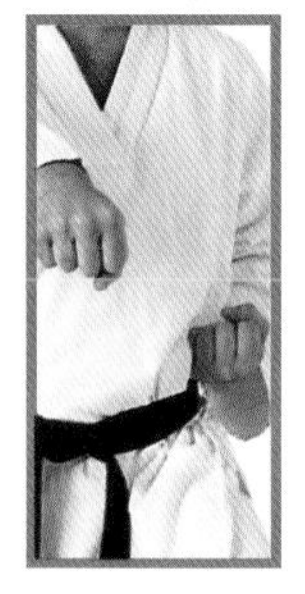

tae kwon do patterns

Tae Kwon Do uses patterns in a similar way to that in which Karate uses Kata. To the uninitiated eye, the patterns may look similar. They are actually very different in their movements and the way that the movements are interlaced together.

In Tae Kwon Do there is a greater emphasis upon kicks and a higher centre of gravity when you are training. This is shown from the very beginning by having a front snap kick with both legs in the first pattern and the use of a walking stance, as well as front stance. Long before you reach black belt, you should have an interesting array of kicks in your arsenal.

A common series of patterns in Tae Kwon Do is called the Taeguk sequence, in which there are eight patterns. They are used as a basis for the gradings in one of the larger Tae Kwon Do federations, in a similar way to the Kata in Karate.

The word Taeguk is the Korean name for the yin/yang symbol in the middle of the Korean flag. The flag itself is called Taegukki. The Taeguk symbol represents the idea of two forces that oppose each other, but are in harmony and balance. The idea of yin and yang is therefore integral to the Tae Kwon Do method and is represented in this pattern.

The first pattern, Taeguk 1, is also called Il Jang. Il Jang represents the creative force that is in all physical forms. It is considered to be the fundamental starting point of Tae Kwon Do. These concepts should be understood by the Tae Kwon Do student in order to gain an insight into the 'spirit of Tae Kwon Do'. After that, all you need is hard work and self-discipline.

Taeguk 1

For the purpose of illustrating the movements clearly, moves where the practitioner would turn to the left have been photographed from the front.

1 Start from the Tae Kwon Do ready position.

2 Move the left foot and turn 90° into the walking stance. The left foot leads. Execute a left downward block.

3 Step forward, with your right leg in the walking stance, and punch with your right fist to middle section. (All punches in this form are aimed at the solar plexus.)

4 Move your right foot to turn right to 180°. Finish in the walking stance, with your right foot forward, and execute a downward block with your right arm.

5 Step forward, with your left leg in the walking stance, and then punch with your left fist.

6 Move your left foot and turn 90° into a front stance, with your left foot forward, and execute a left downward block.

7 Immediately follow with a reverse punch with your right fist.

8 Move your right foot, turn 90° into the walking stance and execute a left front block (with your right foot forward).

9 Step forward, with your left foot in the walking stance, and execute a reverse punch with your right fist.

10 Move your left foot to turn 180° into the walking stance, with your left foot forward, and execute a right front block.

11 Step forward with your right foot and execute a left reverse punch to the middle section. Keep right fist close to body.

12 Move your right foot to turn 90° into the front stance, with your right foot forward, and execute a right-arm downward block.

13 Immediately follow with a left middle-section punch.

13 Move your left foot to turn 90° into the walking stance and then execute a left rising block.

14 Execute a right-leg front snap kick.

15 Come down from the kick into a walking stance, with the right foot forward, and execute a right middle-section punch.

16 Move your right foot to turn 180° into the walking stance, with your right foot leading. Perform a front rising block.

17 Execute a left-leg front snap kick.

18 Come down from the kick into the walking stance, with your left foot forward, and execute a left middle-section punch.

19 Move your right leg to turn 90°to your right into a front stance, with your left foot forward. Execute a right downward block.

20 Step forward with your left leg into the front stance and execute a middle-section punch. Yell 'KI-HAP'!

21 Return to the attention position.

kung fu – wing chun style

what is kung fu?

If asked 'What is Kung Fu?' many people would associate it with the dramatic fighting sequences seen in films. The truth of the answer is somewhat different. The phrase is actually difficult to interpret directly into English. A loose translation is that Kung Fu means 'Technical Skill'. The phrase can therefore be used in a much wider context than just the world of martial arts. For example, a chef could have 'good Kung Fu', meaning simply that the chef is a very skilled cook.

The techniques of Win Chun are both simple and effective. There are however, many subtleties that need to be learnt and practiced.

what is wing chun?

The number of different styles of Chinese martial arts is staggering. They include the Shaolin styles demonstrated in recent years in the West by the Shaolin monks, the Animal styles, such as White Crane and Praying Mantis, as well as the various weapon forms.

Some of these forms have become a hybrid mixture of gymnastics and martial arts. This is not to detract from the artistry involved in the style. Some of the less martial styles can look very impressive when performed well. The context of this book, however, is more concerned with the styles that are more practical in the martial sense.

A style that enjoys great popularity is the Wing Chun style. Probably the most famous martial artist of all time was the late Bruce Lee. Wing Chun was a style that Bruce Lee studied to a high level, and he even incorporated some of its ideas into his own style of Jeet Kuen Do.

Wing Chun is a deceptively simple-looking martial art. It contains no strong punches or high kicks. This sometimes repels students from studying the art, as they do not think that it can be effective. It is, however, a complete and effective martial art, with many subtle techniques that will require time and patience to master.

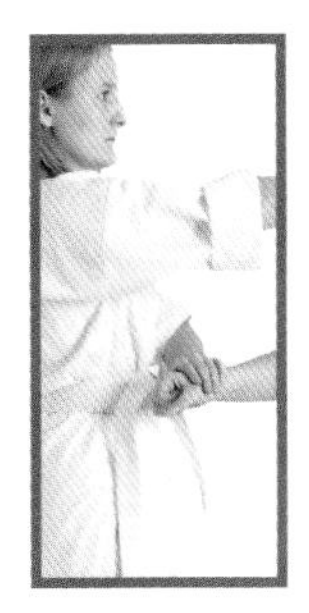

history of wing chun

The story of the origins of Wing Chun starts four-hundred years ago, in the famous Shaolin Temple. The Ming Dynasty had recently been defeated and the conquering Manchurians were seen by many as oppressors. This made the Manchurians dsire to control all power within their country.

The monks at the Shaolin Temple were all very skilled martial artists, and their reputation was widespread. The ruling Qing Dynasty therefore saw the Shaolin Temple as an unacceptable threat and decided to eliminate it.

There were several unsuccessful attacks. The Qing soldiers were unable to defeat the highly skilled monks, but eventually they persuaded one of the monks to join them. He helped them to burn down the temple and many monks were killed.

Some of the monks and nuns escaped. One of these was a nun called Ng Moy. After the burning of the temple, she made her way south to the White Crane Temple to study there.

She also spent time in the mountains looking for medicinal herbs. During this time she befriended a young woman named Yim Wing Chun. Yim Wing Chun was engaged to be married to the man she loved. However, the leader of a local gang also wanted to marry her.

Ng Moy was unable to intervene directly, as this would have attracted the attention of the soldiers who had attacked the Shaolin Temple. She therefore decided to teach Yim Wing Chun her skill in martial arts.

After some time, Yim Wing Chun issued a challenge to the leader of the gang that she would marry him if he could beat her in a fight. The challenge seemed ridiculous, so the leader readily agreed. After she had used her skill to beat not only the leader, but also several of the gang members, Yim Wing Chun was left in peace. She was able to marry the man of her choice and a new martial art was born, to which her name was given.

Although this story has probably been romanticised and embellished, the later developments of Wing Chun are less shrouded by time and are well catalogued for the serious student. The tale of Ng Moy and Yim Wing Chun, however, should be known by any martial artist who enjoys listening to a good story!

The opening of the Wing Chun sequence guards against an attack to the groin and an attack to the neck. Either of these blocks can be easily effected from the starting position, where hands are drawn back into the body at waist height.

is kung fu for me, and what do I need?

The Wing Chun student requires very little equipment to study the art. Most students of Wing Chun will train wearing a T-shirt, jogging pants and often trainers on their feet. More advanced students will also start to learn how to use various weapons. Weapons training will not begin until the student has gained good experience with empty-hand forms and practice.

Wing Chun practice does not assume a high level of fitness at the beginning. It is true that continued practice will improve your fitness and strength, but you should not be dissuaded from studying the art if you do not consider yourself a highly fit person to begin with. Wing Chun is very good for making your legs stronger and improving your posture.

Chi Sau, or 'sticking hands', is an important part of Wing Chun training, and will be explained in more detail later in the chapter. It involves close contact with an opponent, and if you enter a Chi Sau tournament, you stand a chance of receiving some strikes if you let your opponent through your defence. Having said this, there are many Chi Sau competitions with both men and women entrants, and there are few real injuries in these events.

You do not need to be super fit to practice Wing Chun. Regular practice will enhance your fitness, and will help you gain flexibility and stamina. It will also help to optimise your coordination. There is some close contact, as in the Chi Sau movements, but you run very little risk of sustaining an injury.

principles of wing chun

In Wing Chun, and some other martial arts, such as Tai Chi and Pa Kua, it is important to keep your centre line straight. By the centre line, we mean the dividing line that runs vertically through the body (shown below). This sounds simple, but do not forget that your opponent will be trying to upset your centre line.

Why is this important? Consider the Leaning Tower of Pisa. It is leaning because the ground beneath it cannot support its weight properly. It has 'lost its centre'. Without the ingenuity of the engineers who have kept it standing for so long, it would have collapsed a long time ago.

The same is true of the martial artist. If you lose your centre line, then it will be easy for an opponent to topple you. To keep a strong centre line, you need to be like a building with strong foundations. If your legs are strong, then it will be easy for you to keep your centre line and difficult for your opponent to topple you.

Wing Chun uses very close distances for fighting. The inexperienced martial artist will tend to retreat if their opponent is bigger than they are and is using fast techniques. In Wing Chun training, this would be a scenario that you can deal with. If you get close to your opponent, they will not be able to build up the speed or momentum to make their punches and kicks effective. You will therefore be able to control the situation if you have sufficient skill.

You must develop an intuitive sense of where your centre line is, rather than just imagining it in your mind.

quigong and wing chun

Have you ever seen or met one of those old martial arts' masters who seem to have stopped ageing? If you have, you will most likely have noticed that even though their hair may be white, their skin is still soft, their backs are straight and they posses the mental speed of a person who is a quarter of their age.

What is their secret? Apart from good luck, some of this vitality will have come from the fact that they have studied some form of internal training or Quigong. Quigong is a method of relaxing your body and preserving its energy. It is currently enjoying great popularity in the West because of its many benefits.

Wing Chun is a complete martial arts' system. As such, it must have an element of Quigong, or energy-building, integrated into it. The first section of Siu Lim Tao, the Wing Chun pattern, fulfils this requirement.

Try practising it as slowly as you can. Keep your body in motion, but slow the motion down as far as you can. At first this will seem very difficult, or even ridiculous. Do not lose sight of the fact that you are connecting yourself to the inner training that is a part of Wing Chun training. Here you can see the kind of slow, steady movements required (steps 1 to 3).

Try to develop a routine. Set yourself realistic goals and you will find that this style of training will improve your skill. It is another of the dualities of martial arts that the slowest practice can sometimes equate to the fastest learning time.

1

2

3

gong lik and fa ging

The pattern Siu Lim Tao is designed to teach you the basic skills of the style. There are various techniques and applications involved. There are two concepts within the movements that you need to be aware of if you are trying to understand how the sequence works. These are Gong Lik and Fa Ging.

Gong Lik is easiest to understand by example, and this need not necessarily apply to martial arts. It describes a person with a great skill in some type of movement that has been gained through long and hard practice.

An example is the darts player. If an expert darts player throws a dart, they do not try to calculate the fine detail of the darts path. The player knows where the dart will go because the movement is so well practiced. He or she simply has to stay relaxed and let their practice guide them with their actions.

The same is true of the movements of the martial artist. If you are well practiced, you do not need to aim a punch. That would simply slow you down. Your practice will have taught your instincts where the punch will land without you having to stop and aim.

Fa Ging is the application of explosive energy to a technique. In practice, the form may be gentle and flowing, but without the skill of being able to apply the explosive energy it will have no martial value.

The explosive energy from Fa Ging is generated from the Tan Tien (energy centre) that is located in the middle of your abdomen. If you can control your Fa Ging properly, it will involve the whole of your body, and will not simply mean that you are moving your arms quickly.

Advanced students will practise 'sticking legs', as well as 'sticking hands'.

siu lim tao - the wing chun form

Siu Lim Tao is one of the Wing Chun forms. It has similarities to other martial forms in that it is designed to teach you the essence of the movement within the style. One of the differences from other forms is that once you have stepped into the Wing Chun training position there is no other footwork.

This is not to say that you do not use your legs. One of the common aspects of any of the Chinese martial arts' systems is that you need to develop strong legs so that you can create a firm base to stand upon.

An advantage of the minimal footwork is that you will need very little space to practise in. This could be a big advantage to somebody who lives in the city and will probably not have much room for practising.

The form Siu Lim Tao will be shown here by demonstrating the beginning of the first section. There are many more movements to the form and it could easily fill a book trying to explain the whole of the sequence.

The first form

Starting movement

1 Start by standing with your feet together and your arms relaxed. Keep your head upright and your back straight. Look forward, but do not stare at anything. Let your breathing become soft and deep. Let your mind become still and do not allow any outside thoughts to enter it. If you can relax your mind your body will relax. If your body can relax it will allow your mind to relax further.

2 Make fists with your hands and raise them to your chest. Your forearms should be parallel to the floor. Do not rest your fists on your body.

3 Point the toes of your right foot outwards and move your foot to the side. Touch down with your toes and push your heel out further, so that your heels are wider apart than your toes. Your feet should be a shoulder width apart.

4 Sink your weight by bending your knees. Keep your back straight. This is the resting position for the Wing Chun fist and is returned to many times if you complete the whole of the form.

Keep your back straight and keep looking forwards. Do not rise up and down when you are opening the stance. Let the weight of your waist sink and support yourself with your thigh muscles. Breathe slowly and evenly through your nose. This is the basic Wing Chun training position.

Marking the centre line

The importance of understanding your own, and your opponent's, centre line was discussed earlier. You need to be able to understand your own centre line before you can work with that of others.

The movement could also be used as a lower block followed by an upper block.

1 Cross your hands in front of your body. The point where your wrists cross should be above your Tan Tien (in front of the lower abdomen). The right arm should be inside the left arm.

2 Raise your hands in front of your chest, so that the wrists cross in front of your upper chest and throat. This is also covering an important energy centre called Hsuan Chi – the throat energy centre.

The path of your hands will mark your centre line, so your forearms will have to roll to execute this movement.

3 Draw your hands back into the resting position.

Chung kuen – centre-line punch

This style of punch generates explosive power (Fa Ging) by moving inwards to the centre line to torque the waist. If you simply throw a punch without moving your waist you will generate very little power.

1 Bring your left fist into the centre of your chest. Prepare to strike.

2 Punch with the knuckles of your fist facing forward. At this point the movement travels outwards in a straight line and finishes with your arm in a straight, not locked, position.

Note that the next movement (p82) teaches you how to withdraw the fist. Do not simply pull it back to where it started from.

Withdrawing the fist

1 Open your fist so that your palm faces upwards.

2 Relax your hand so that it curls. Rotate the wrist inwards, in a clockwise direction, as far as you can. Remember to keep your shoulders relaxed.

3 Continue the movement by extending your fingers and then pull them back into a fist.

4 Bring your fist back into the resting position.

Repeat the centre-line punch and withdrawing the fist for the right hand.

chi sau - sticking hands

There is little point in learning the movements of a martial art pattern if you never train with other people. You will never know if you have martial skill if you never test it in some way with a training partner. This means that there needs to be a safe way of practising the techniques.

In Wing Chun there is such a method of training, and it is called Chi Sau. Chi Sau literally translates into 'sticking hands'. The translation from the Chinese language to the English language actually works quite well here.

Chi Sau is designed to teach you how to be sensitive to your partner's movements so that you can follow them, or 'stick' to your partner. You will move with the flow of your partner's movement in order to try to use your technique to gain the best position.

If you learn Chi Sau, you will start by learning a set sequence of movements that will teach you how to flow with your opponent. When you have mastered single-handed sticking hands you will move on to double-handed sticking hands and then bring your legs into the equation to practise your kicks. This level of skill will give the whole of your body a workout and will improve your balance immensely.

When you have become adept at the sequences from sticking hands, you will start to do a 'freestyle' sticking hands. This is where you will use the techniques from Wing Chun, but will use the sequence that you see fit in order to get through your partner's defence.

Single-handed sticking hands

1 When you make contact, you will try to keep the contact by 'sticking'.

2 If your hand is in the upper position, then you can open an attack.

3 Your partner will try to roll around your arm to gain the upper position.

Double-handed sticking hands

1 When you have mastered single-handed sticking hands, you will be ready for double-handed sticking hands.

2 You will again be trying to feel through your partner's guard to open an attack.

Sticking feet

This more advanced level will give you greater strength in your legs. It enables you to force your opponent off-balance.

Parry and strike

When you have penetrated your partner's defence, you can strike. A blow to the head is usually very effective!

Guarding block

The guarding block is a typical Wing Chun fighting stance. It is an effective way to prepare for attack.

Inch punch

The most famous technique from Wing Chun is the 'Inch punch' that Bruce Lee was able to demonstrate so effectively. It was thought by many to be similar to a conjuring trick because it is executed from such a small distance that it seems that there can be no power in it.

The mistake that is commonly made with the Inch punch is to watch the hand only. In fact, the energy from the punch is actually issued by using the whole body. When performing the punch your body has to be very soft – relaxed – except at the exact moment of impact. It will require much practice in order to master the technique, as the timing is crucial.

2 The fist clenches and is driven forward by the waist. All of your energy should be focused into that split second of impact. After the impact, your body should relax again.

1 The fingers are placed lightly on the chest. You should be very relaxed.

ju jitsu

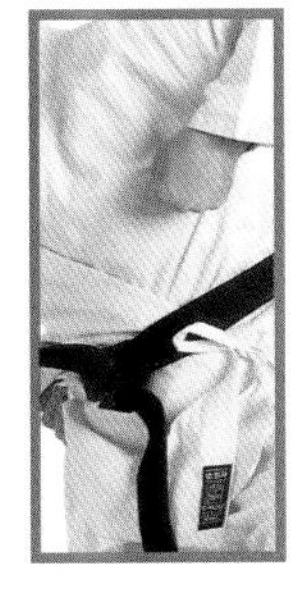

what is ju jitsu?

'By any means necessary' could be a way of summing up the basic philosophy of Ju Jitsu. If we add 'by the minimum possible force' to the statement, then we are approaching the rationale behind the style. The Ju Jitsu style is both efficient and dangerous.

Ju Jitsu literally translates as to 'the art of softness'. Do not be deceived by this definition. The 'softness' referred to here is concerning the need for the Ju Jitsu student to stay relaxed and in control.

Traditional Ju Jitsu contains many techniques that could easily cause fatal or serious injury if used in the wrong way. With such an array of techniques at their disposal it is important for the student to understand a strict code of discipline. The name for this code is Bushido, or the 'way of the warrior'.

This code must influence the student's daily life, as well as their combat skills. Otherwise there would be a serious risk that unsuitable people could be taught some very dangerous techniques. The daily-life aspect of this code can also be the background for such studies as Zen Buddhism.

Many Ju Jitsu techniques are very dangerous, and should be respected as such.

history of ju jitsu

Ju Jitsu is one of the oldest of the Japanese martial arts. It could indeed be argued that all Japanese martial arts have at least some of their roots in Ju Jitsu. This helps to explain why it covers such a wide range of techniques. Strikes, joint locks and throws are all used in Ju Jitsu.

As with any of the older martial arts, the beginnings have become shrouded in legend. Many of the references have indeed been flavoured by the storyteller's individual tastes in martial arts. Some of the old Japanese chronicles give reference to Ju Jitsu as starting in pre-Christian times.

When you have thrown your opponent, you will always finish them with an attack to a vital area.

Many of the throws in Ju Jitsu are similar to Judo throws.

is ju jitsu for me, and what do I need?

Ju Jitsu can theoretically be practised by almost any able-bodied person. However, you should consider whether you have the right temperament for this particular art. Ju Jitsu contains many techniques that will cause some discomfort when practised. If you simply cannot endure practising such movements as strangleholds and joint locks, then maybe you should consider another style.

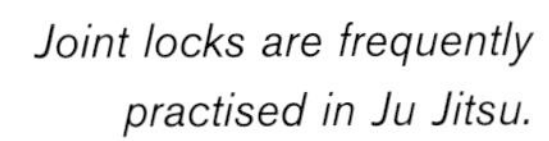
Joint locks are frequently practised in Ju Jitsu.

Ju Jitsu is not a sport. If you would like to try a style in which you can enter tournaments and try to win medals, then traditional Ju Jitsu is probably not for you. Judo, Tae Kwon Do or Karate may be more suitable if you wish to test yourself in this type of arena.

Bowing is a sign of respect. You would always bow to your opponent before beginning a tournament.

belts and grading

The journey through Ju Jitsu has the following belts and gradings

7th Kyu	White (red stripe)
6th Kyu	Yellow
5th Kyu	Orange
4th Kyu	Green
3rd Kyu	Blue
2nd Kyu	Purple
1st Kyu	Brown
Shodan ho	Black and brown
1st to 5th Dan	Black

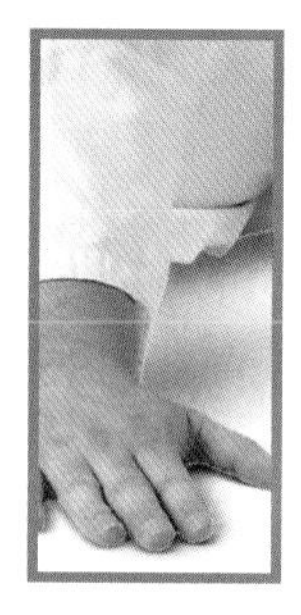

etiquette

Etiquette is of vital importance when studying any martial art. Respect for the art and all of the masters and students who have trained before you is a cornerstone for the Bushido way. If you cannot respect your classmates and teachers, then how can you learn from them?

This mutual respect is in some ways the first part of removing the egotistical behaviour that can be so dangerous when learning martial arts. This discipline is vital as it prepares and calms the mind, as well as demonstrating respect both for your opponent, and for the martial art itself.

Rei ● kneeling bow

At the beginning and the end of your lesson you will normally be expected to perform the kneeling bow (Rei). This is comprised of several stages, as follows.

1 Begin by standing to attention, with your feet together and your palms resting lightly by your thighs.

2 Lower your left knee to the mat. Keep your back straight.

4 Slide your hands forward on the mat so that your body leans forward. Look at your instructor, not the mat. Pause briefly in the lowest position.

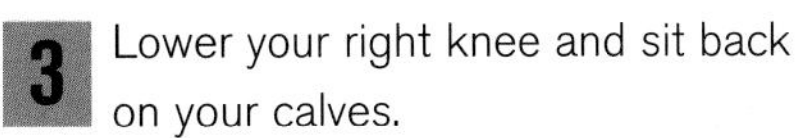

3 Lower your right knee and sit back on your calves.

5 Return to the standing position by raising the left knee and then the right. Perform a standing bow to your instructor.

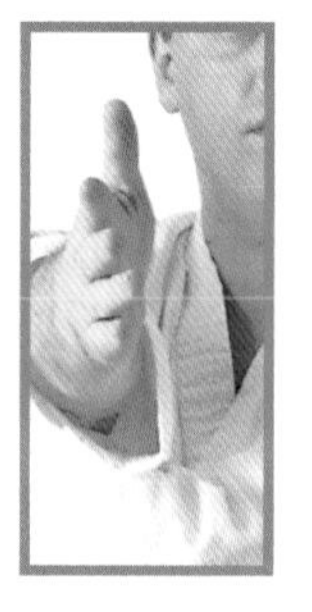

ju jitsu exercises

In Ju Jitsu there are many attacks and counterattacks that involve the use of wrist locks. It makes sense that if you are going to practise such techniques you should be able to loosen the joints in your wrists and arms. This will help you to train for longer without having to stop.

Wrist exercise 1

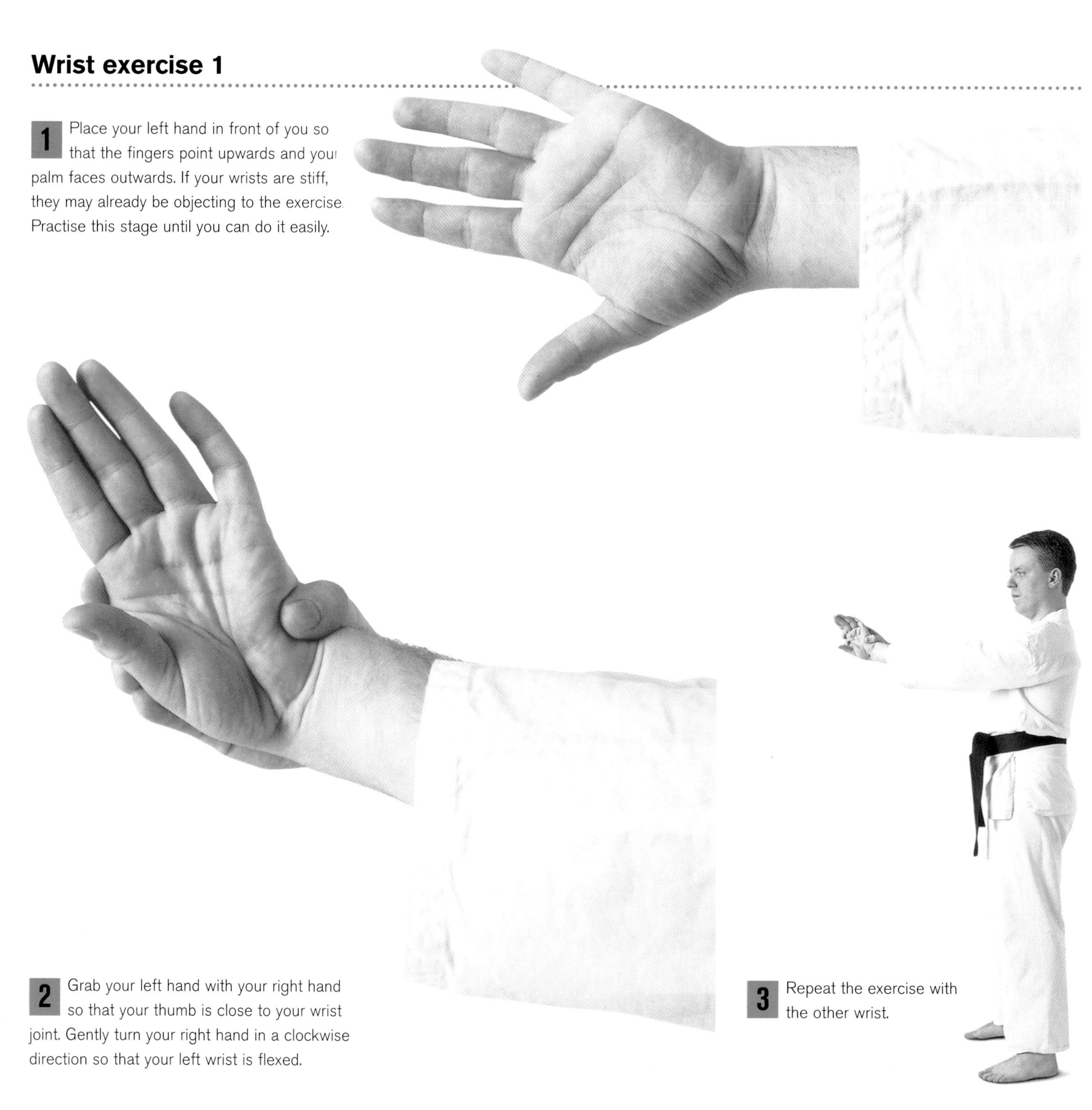

1 Place your left hand in front of you so that the fingers point upwards and your palm faces outwards. If your wrists are stiff, they may already be objecting to the exercise. Practise this stage until you can do it easily.

2 Grab your left hand with your right hand so that your thumb is close to your wrist joint. Gently turn your right hand in a clockwise direction so that your left wrist is flexed.

3 Repeat the exercise with the other wrist.

Wrist exercise 2

1 Place your left hand in front of you in a similar way to the first exercise, except that your forearm is turned the other way.

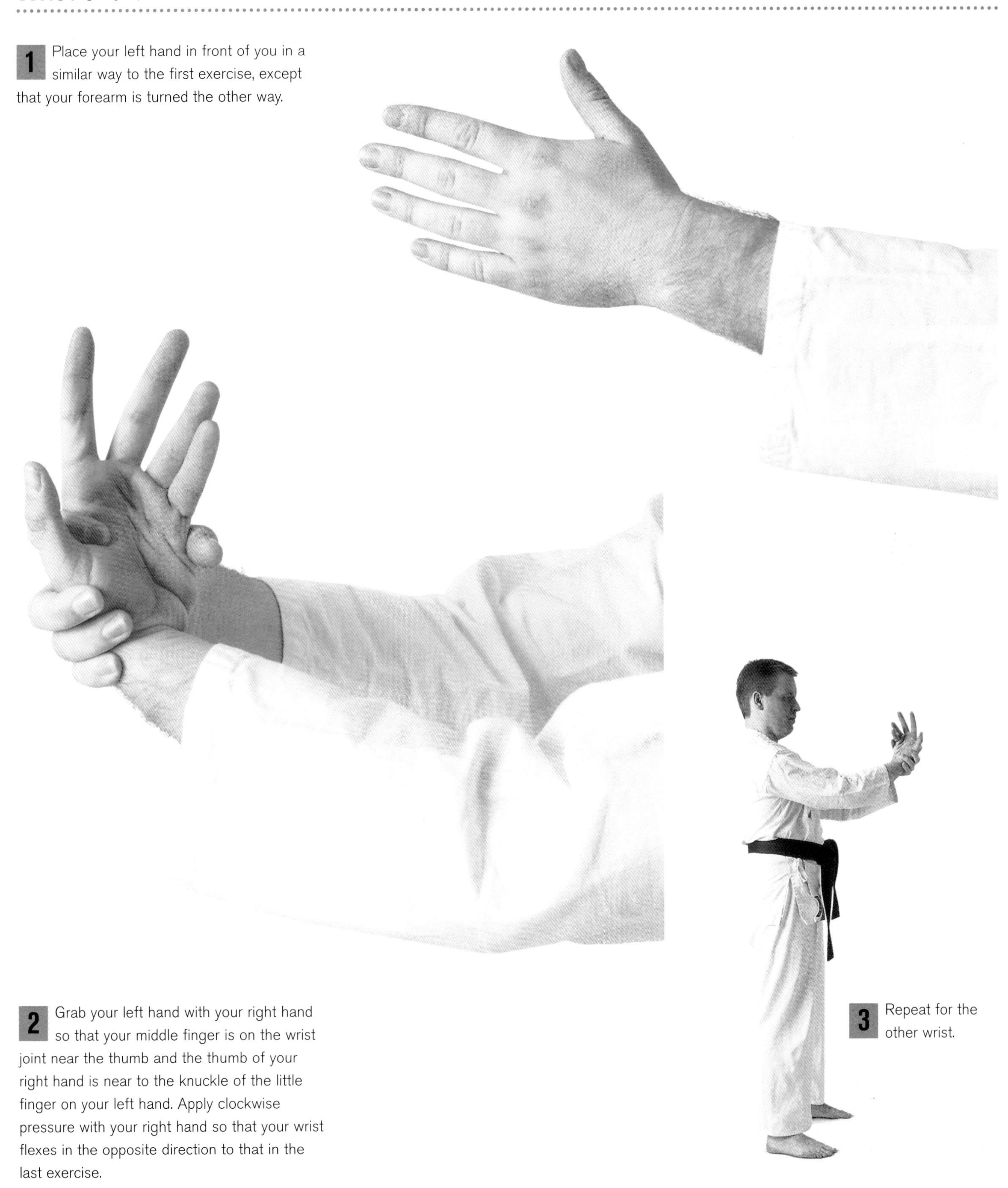

2 Grab your left hand with your right hand so that your middle finger is on the wrist joint near the thumb and the thumb of your right hand is near to the knuckle of the little finger on your left hand. Apply clockwise pressure with your right hand so that your wrist flexes in the opposite direction to that in the last exercise.

3 Repeat for the other wrist.

Shoulder and elbow exercise

N.B. This sequence requires that the joints in the arms are fairly supple in the first place. If you experience any pain or difficulty, consult your instructor.

1 Extend your right arm in front of you. Keep your left arm at your side.

2 Raise your left forearm in front of your right elbow.

3 Apply pressure with your left forearm so that your right arm is pulled and the right shoulder is stretched. Hold for 10 seconds.

4 Relax the grip and bend your right arm at the elbow so that you can grab your right hand with your left.

5 Press down gently with your left hand so that your right arm is stretched. Hold for 10 seconds.

Break falls

One aspect that Ju Jitsu shares with Judo is the practice of break falls. Both systems use the same type of break falls. Some variations may occur between different associations, but the important thing to remember is how to perform the technique.

We can therefore state that for the purposes of the beginner, the break falls in Judo and Ju Jitsu are interchangeable. When you become more advanced, the only real difference is concerned with how you come out of the break fall in a way that sets you up for the next move.

We shall consider the side break fall and the back break fall in this section. Remember that if you practise break falls you should have crash mats under you to prevent injury.

Side break fall

When you have become competent in the side break fall from the squatting position shown, then you can gradually increase the height that you practise from. Practise on both sides. Practise the most on the side that you find the most difficult. This will force you to analyse the technique to a deeper level and increase your understanding of both sides.

1 Begin from a crouching position and stretch both arms in front of you.

2 Overbalance to the left and slap the mat with your left forearm. This slap will take some of the kinetic energy out of the fall. Keep your body relaxed. If your body is loose and relaxed it is less likely to sustain damage than if it is tense.

The right knee should lift to protect the groin and your right hand should be ready to counterattack or guard your head.

3 Once you are down, you are not out! Counterattack by aiming a Karate-style side kick to your opponent's knee.

Back break fall

As with the side break fall, you should start from a low, squatting position and gradually increase to a standing position as you become more proficient and confident.

1 Begin from a crouching position and stretch both arms in front of you.

2 Roll back along the curve of your spine. You should tuck your chin to your chest and curve your back to make a circular shape that will not need to absorb any impact.

As you land, you should slap both of your forearms on the mat to absorb the impact of the fall. Finish with both feet on the mat.

3 A good counterattack from this position is to place a front snap kick to your imaginary opponent's groin. That should make them think twice, imaginary or not!

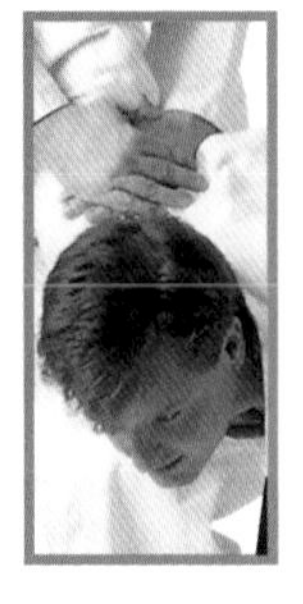

ju jitsu techniques

Ju Jitsu contains a vast array of techniques. The following are a selection of the easiest, and the ones that you are most likely to learn if you start a class. Remember that you should never practise these techniques unless you are with a qualified teacher, in order to avoid injuring yourself and your partner.

Wrist lock

This is a basic technique upon which many more complicated techniques are built. Remember not to use too much force when practising with a training partner.

1 Your partner has tried to grab you with their right hand. This lock is also ideal to deal with other techniques that lead with the hand, such as a punch or a push.

2 Use your left hand to grab your partner's right hand, using an overhand grip.

3 Turn your partner's wrist until their hand faces them. Bring your right hand in to strengthen the grip. Your partner is now entirely at your mercy.

4 Finish them off by applying force to the wrist joint so that they are forced down to their knees.

Recumbent ankle throw

A part of the Bushido way is never to give up. Just because you are on the floor does not mean that you are beaten. This throw is a technique that demonstrates how dangerous you can be, even after you have lost your balance.

1 You are on the floor and your partner is standing. Hook your left instep over their left shin.

2 Thrust your right foot at your opponent's knee. Use the side kick to hit your opponent's knee. This will trip your opponent over your foot.

3 Show them to think twice the next time by delivering a snap kick to the groin.

Escape from a rear grab

1 Your opponent has grabbed you from behind.

2 Drop your weight by bending your knees. Raise your elbows to loosen their grip. As you feel the grip loosen, step back with your right foot and grab their knee.

3 Stand up quickly and pull up their knee, so that they tip over backwards, and drop them to the floor.

4 Drop to your knees and punch your opponent in the groin.

Escape from a ground strangle

1 Your opponent is trying to strangle you from behind while you are prone.

2 Grab both of their ears. This should make him start releasing his hold.

3 Pull their ears down as you bring your knee into their face. That should do the trick!

Your first grading

After you have become skilled in the basic techniques, your instructor will enter you for your grading. You will be required to demonstrate a thorough knowledge of the techniques in order to pass the grading.

I have outlined some of the basic techniques that you will need to pass your first grading. This is not intended to be a comprehensive manual to get you through that grading, however. It is more of a snapshot of what you will have to do to get through the grading.

Escape from rear strangle

1 Your opponent tries to attack you from behind with a stranglehold.

2 Step to the left and strike them in the groin with the back of your hand. This will probably be enough to make them let go, but you need to control the situation and they are going to be angry after what you have done.

3 Your opponent is stunned from the blow to the groin. This will make it easy for you to throw them over your leg.

4 Take hold of their arm so that they cannot escape. Bring your right hand to your hip in preparation for a punch.

5 Keep hold of their arm with one hand and punch their temple with the other.

6 Take your opponent's arm and put them into a wrist lock. Hold their body firmly by digging one knee into their neck and the other into their lower rib.

Escape From Strangle

1 Your opponent grabs you around the neck to attempt a stranglehold.

2 Swing your hips away from your attacker. Use this hip movement to drive your right forearm across you in a blocking style of movement. This will break your opponent's hold on you. Continue the momentum of the swing so that your fist comes near to your ear.

3 Strike your opponent with a back fist strike. You should aim to strike your opponent on the side of their jaw.

Straight armlock

1 Your opponent tries to punch you in the stomach. Block downwards with your left hand.

2 Grab your opponent's punching hand with your right hand and raise your left hand over their elbow.

3 Keep hold of their hand and swivel around on your left foot so that you are facing the same way as your opponent. Simultaneously drop your left arm.

4 Hook your left arm under your opponent's elbow and lift it. Press down on their extended hand to engage the lock fully. This still leaves their other hand free, but they are unlikely to try to punch because they will be more concerned about the arm that you have just put into the lock.

Shoulder lock

1 Your opponent is trying to attack you with a punch to your stomach with their right hand. Use a downward block to remove the threat of the punch.

2 Move your opponent's right arm in a circle to their back. Place your right hand on your opponent's shoulder.

3 Trap your opponent's arm against your left shoulder and press down on their shoulder with both hands. This will fully engage your opponent in a shoulder lock.

4 Finish your opponent with a swift front snap kick to their face. This will certainly render him harmless!

what is tai chi?

Tai Chi is a soft, or internal, martial art. This means that all of the movements will be in circular patterns and there will be a great importance upon internal, or 'energy,' training. For this reason, Tai Chi is practised by many healers. It helps you to centre and refine your own energy before you try to help others.

It should not be assumed that 'soft' means that there is no martial application. A well-known Tai Chi master was given the nickname 'Invincible', because of his great proficiency in the martial aspect of Tai Chi.

Tai Chi is practised slowly, so that you can teach your body the exact postures and alignments that will give you strength in your posture. This is a useful tip for any martial artist. Try practising a front kick from Tae Kwon Do or Karate at a very slow speed and you will soon understand the mental and physical stamina required for this type of training.

Internal and external co-ordination are required for Tai Chi practice.

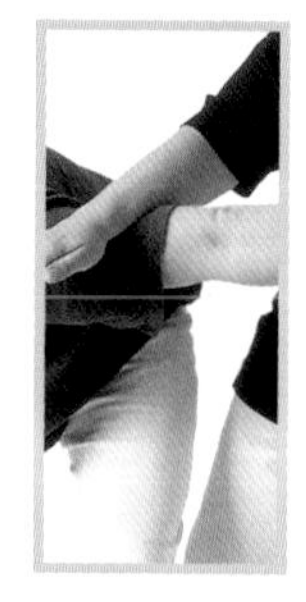

history of tai chi

Some of the stories about Tai Chi and its origins are more entertaining than believable. The reason for this is that Tai Chi has become embedded within the folk traditions of China. Some of the stories have been passed down from father to son and have gained a few embellishments along the way. This is the only way to view the story of a swordsman being beaten when his intended victim, who happened to be a Tai Chi master, did not even wake up!

Some of the folk stories also contain a seed of wisdom, however. A common story of the origins of Tai Chi is that a Taoist monk was watching a crane trying to catch a snake. The lithe and supple movements of the snake allowed it to escape to frustrate another crane. This story illustrates how the softness of the snake allowed it to avoid becoming the crane's next meal.

The first usage of the words 'Tai Chi' was in the *I-Ching*, or 'Book of Changes', dating from the Zhou Dynasty (221 BC). Tai Chi in this sense refers to the two opposites that are frequently referred to as yin and yang.

Chen Wanting, who lived in the 16th century, is considered by many to be the 'father' of Tai Chi. He served as a royal guard in his home village and was taught by a famous general in the imperial army. After the fall of the Ming Dynasty, Chen Wanting withdrew from society to further his Taoist studies. He wrote many manuscripts and taught his art to other people.

The 18th century saw the rise of Yang Luchan (1799–1872). He was born to a poor family and left home as a child to become a servant for the Chen family. Yang Luchan would watch and learn from the martial arts' instructors around him. After very hard training he, too, became a skilled martial artist.

Yang adapted the style that he had learned so that it became more accessible to ordinary people. The Yang style of Tai Chi was then born. The style was later adapted by his son, Yang Jianhou, and his grandson, Yang Chengfu. The Yang Chengfu form is the one that is practised by the modern school of Yang practitioners.

The Wu style was invented by another of Yang Luchan's sons, Yang Banhou. This style of Tai Chi uses a slightly different way of moving, but is otherwise similar in its method.

Many of the Tai Chi techniques have been passed down through several generations.

is tai chi for me, and what do I need?

Tai Chi can be learned by anybody. The slow and gentle movements do not put your body under any undue stress. The movements will build up your inner strength with little risk of injury. It has been used in this way throughout history both to prevent and aid recovery from illness and to reduce stress.

If you prefer the idea of a quick-moving martial art, with aspects such as high-jumping kicks and sparring, Tai Chi may not be what you require at present. Likewise, if your main focus at the moment is to improve your fighting skills, you should look at other styles first.

Tai Chi takes years to learn and a lifetime to master. Some aspects will take days for one person to understand and years for another. You can rest assured, however, that the person who has learned one part quickly will soon find something that will challenge them more. This is why Tai Chi teachers generally do not use a grading system such as belts. Tai Chi forces you to turn your concentration inwards, to your own development.

Tai Chi can employ explosive movements to throw your opponent back from you.

energy-building exercises, tai chi circle and zhan zhuang

Energy-building exercises give you a new understanding of your body.

Within the style of Tai Chi there are many bodily requirements that are closely linked with emotional and mental requirements. Two constant requirements are 'letting go' and internal energy, or Chi.

A useful exercise for teaching your body to 'let go' of unwanted tension is the Tai Chi circle. The 'standing like a tree', or Zhan Zhuang, exercise is a simple, but very effective, way of nurturing your internal energy.

Tai Chi circle

At top sporting events you will frequently see the contestants performing some sort of deep-breathing exercise before an event. One of the reasons for this is that it helps you to clear your mind and 'let go' of the outside world. This phenomenon has been noticed by the Taoists and has been developed into the next exercise.

For this exercise, all of the breathing is done through your nose, and your position remains stationary. Try to empty your mind and to keep your body relaxed.

1 Stand with your feet parallel and a shoulder width apart. Look straight in front of you, but do not stare at anything.

2 Turn your hands so that the palms face outwards. Continue to look straight ahead.

3 On an inward breath, raise both of your hands in a circle. Keep your shoulders down and synchronise the movement of your hands with your breathing.

Zhan Zhuang

The next exercise looks easy, but do not be fooled by appearances. It is a very powerful and intense way of building your inner energy, or Chi. Most people will find that after what seems like only a short period of time they will have to stop.

The secret is to build up the length of practice time over a period of time. This will build up your inner-body strength and improve your posture in a way that is beneficial to your health and to your martial arts' practice.

1 Start with your feet a shoulder width apart and parallel. Keep your back straight, head upright, eyes alert, but not fixed, and relax your breathing.

2 Bend your knees slightly, as though you were resting your buttocks on the edge of a table. At the same time, keep your head up and your back straight.

3 Bring your arms up in front of your chest. Do not raise your shoulders and try to stay relaxed.

Hold the position for as long as is comfortable. Keep your breathing soft and relaxed. When you have practised a few times, you can start to build up a training schedule around your practice times.

The phrase 'Zhan Zhuang' literally means 'standing like a tree'. Imagine that you are the tree and that you are growing from within.

4 When your hands reach the top of the circle, lower your shoulders and elbows and then press your palms down gently with an outward breath.

Start the movement again. Keep it as slow and relaxed as possible, so that your breathing becomes deeper. Some Tai Chi masters can perform this exercise at the speed of three repetitions per minute and will still not be short of breath.

basic techniques – ward off, roll back, squeeze and push

If you decide to learn Tai Chi, then you will learn a sequence of movements. For these movements to become Tai Chi, and not a form of dance, they must be done with 'intent'. This means that you will need to understand the movements rather than simply performing them

Within the Tai Chi form are four basic techniques that cover the majority of the movements. These basic techniques are ward off, roll back, squeeze and push. When you learn a new part of a sequence, whether it be 'carry tiger to the mountain', from the Yang style, or 'ride the animal in the reverse direction', from the Chen style, it will be possible to analyse it in terms of the main techniques.

Ward off

Ward off is the most common technique within the Yang style. It is aptly named because the name implies exactly what it is used for. The main use of ward off is for blocking or intercepting an opponent's strike. Here you see two examples of how effective such a defence can be.

It is used in this way for 'waving hands like clouds' and 'kick with heel', amongst others.

Roll back

Roll back is frequently used to follow ward off. It is usually used to control the opponent after the attack has been neutralised with ward off. The examples show the single- and the double-handed techniques.

Roll back is used in this way for 'waving hands like clouds' and 'apparent close-up'.

Squeeze

Squeeze is a very strong movement that is usually performed with two hands within the form. It can be used as a deflection, or literally to bounce your opponent out of the way if you have been able to develop the technique well enough.

The main usage of squeeze in the Yang style is within the commonly repeated sequence 'grasping the sparrow's tail'. If used in the way described, it can help you to develop a real sense of Tai Chi 'rooting'.

The squeeze technique can make a strong defence.

By pushing back on your opponent you can place them in a very vulnerable position.

Try adopting a strong squeeze posture and get a training partner to push against it. You should be able to withstand a considerable amount of force. If you find that you are collapsing in a certain part of your body, stop the practice. The point where you start to collapse is the weakest part of your posture. Realign yourself and try again. After some practice it is surprising how strong the posture actually is.

Push

Push is the main striking movement within Tai Chi. It uses the same bodily requirements if it is done with an open palm or a closed fist.

The heel kicks can also be regarded as pushes that have been executed with the foot instead of the hand.

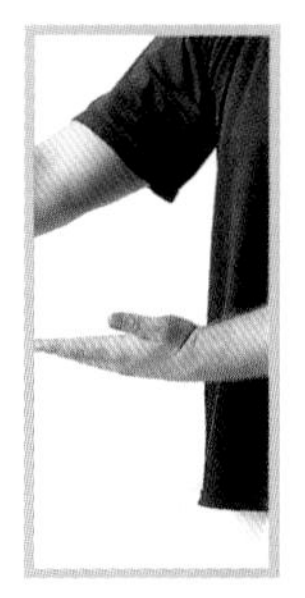

tai chi form practice

Tai Chi forms are usually easy to recognise from the fact that they are usually practised quite slowly. The main reason for this is that it helps your body to learn the movements in a very precise and yet relaxed way. The movements will look graceful because of the circular motion.

The sequence shown here is from the first part of the traditional Yang style. The remainder of the form is equally graceful, and it is well worth studying the full form to get a true picture of how the movements flow.

The sequence of movements will be:

1. opening form
2. grasping the sparrow's tail
3. single whip.

This sequence repeats itself many times during the traditional Yang-style form, and is the bedrock of the sequence. Remember the movements should flow smoothly – do not jerk.

Opening form

This opening movement is just as much a part of the form as any other. It is frequently dismissed as simply the raising and lowering of the arms. The person who performs the form in that way will miss out a vital ingredient – 'intent'.

Keep your head up, back straight and spirit strong for the movement, and it will give you a good start for the rest of the form.

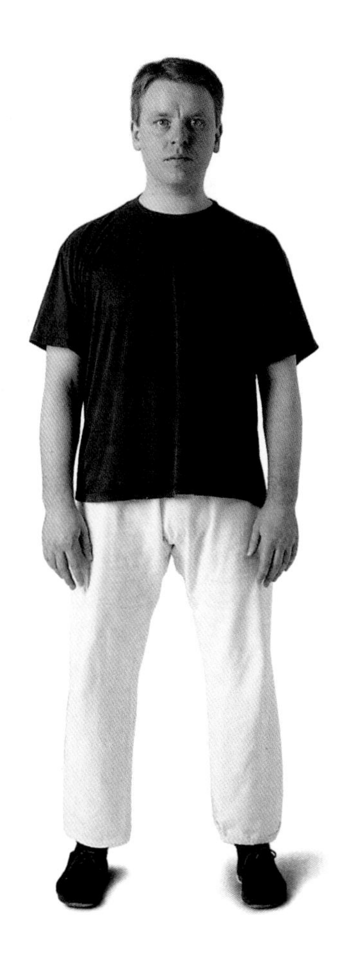

1 Stand with your feet a shoulder width apart and parallel. Your arms should be relaxed and hanging loose in front of your body.

2 Extend your fingers and, on an inward breath, raise your hands to slightly lower than shoulder level.

3 On the outward breath, lower your shoulders, elbows and then the palms of your hands. Keep your fingers pointing forward.

Grasping the sparrow's tail

The sequence called 'grasping the sparrow's tail' is of primary importance within the Yang style. It contains the four basic energies, or movements, within the Tai Chi form (ward off, roll back, squeeze and push).

This explains why the sequence is frequently repeated within the form. If you ever enter a Tai Chi competition where your form is judged, make sure that you can perform this movement well. Without an understanding of this part of the sequence, there can be no understanding of the sequence as a whole.

'Grasping the sparrow's tail' is divided into five different parts. These are:

1. ward off to the left
2. ward off to the right
3. roll back
4. squeeze
5. press.

For the purpose of illustrating the movements clearly, moves where the practitioner would turn to the left have been photographed from the front.

Ward off to the left

1 Continue from the last movement (opening form). Turn your body to the right and shift your weight on to your right leg.

2 Step forward with your left leg. Raise your left arm and circle with the right for a downward press.

3 Look to your right.

Ward off to the right

Turn your body 90° to the right. Do this by shifting your weight on to your right leg and then your left as you turn your body. Step forward with your right leg, place your right arm in front of you and press down with your left hand.

Squeeze

Turn your body back to the centre and place your left hand on the inner forearm of your right arm.
Press your arms forward using the whole of your body.

Roll back

Rotate your body to the right and open your arms.
When your arms have opened, turn your body to the left. Pull back with your left elbow and push with your right hand.

Press

Square your body to separate your arms. Sink your weight on to your back leg, so that your arms are drawn back to your body.
Press forward from your back leg so that you push with your open hands.
Note that there are no changes in footwork between the movements ward off to the left and press.

Single whip

'Single whip' derives its name from the whip-like action of the left arm if the technique is performed at high speed. To be able to perform this whip action, your arm needs to be relaxed, but filled with 'intent'. This is a typical aspect of all Tai Chi movements.

1 Turn your body to the left and rotate your right foot. Put all of your weight on to your left leg.

2 Transfer your weight on to your right leg and turn your body to the right.

3 Form a hook with your right hand and turn your left hand so that your palm faces you. Lift your left heel.

4 Step with your left leg and make your left arm follow your left leg. Place your left foot on the floor, but do not put your weight on to that leg yet.

5 Push your weight from your right leg to your leg and extend your left arm. The right arm should also be extended.

martial arts' applications of the Tai Chi form

All movements within the form should be demonstrated as martial arts' movements.

When learning the martial art aspect of Tai Chi, there are many different ways of interpreting the movements. Usually a defensive movement can also be used as an attacking movement and vice versa. This is the reason why one teacher or book may vary significantly from another. The main rule of thumb here is to use your common sense. If you are being shown a technique that you cannot imagine working, do not believe it until you have had it explained properly or demonstrated.

Within the Yang style of Tai Chi every movement has a martial application. Here we will show some of the possibilities of the sequence as far as the 'single whip' movement that we have reached in our snapshot.

Opening form

1 Your training partner has simulated an attack on you by grabbing your wrists.

2 You respond by extending your fingertips and raising your hands to shoulder height.

3 If you can stay relaxed, you will use the whole of your body to raise your arms and your training partner will be thrown away from you. When you have perfected the technique, you will not use muscular force.

Ward off to the left

1 Your training partner directs a punch or tries to grab you with their right hand.

2 Step forward with your left leg and practise the ward-off manoeuvre shown above.

3 This will lock your training partner's right arm so that it may no longer be used.

4 If you can push against their shoulder joint, you will take away their centre line. This will make it very difficult for them to keep balanced. It will also make it difficult for them to strike you with their right hand, so you will have gained control of your training partner.

Ward off to the right

Another way of controlling the same sort of attack with the opponent's left hand would be to use ward off to the right. This shows that you can use either arm to ward off the attack.

1 When your opponent strikes, you will need to step forward quickly with your right leg. Use your left hand to redirect the attack and place the inside of your elbow on your training partner's elbow.

2 You should slide your left hand down to control your opponent's wrist.

3 If you have control of their wrist and elbow, you can control their whole arm. This will make it impossible for the attacker to continue with the offensive.

Roll back

1 If your opponent or training partner were to feel you trying to catch them in an elbow lock, they would try to escape. In Tai Chi, you always 'go with the flow', so you will not try to hold them solid at this point.

2 The only available route of escape for your training partner is to lift their elbow.

3 When their elbow rises, you will raise your hands with it. There will be a point where your opponent's elbow will not lift any more. This is the moment when you should turn your body to the left and move your arms into the roll-back position.

This forces your opponent's arm into a very awkward position and you will have gained control.

Squeeze

Squeeze makes use of an arm in the ward-off position to push an opponent away. It would be difficult to push somebody using a ward-off arm position in isolation. To make the movement stronger for this type of application, place the palm of your left hand near the inner wrist of your right hand.

This type of arm configuration is known as squeeze. It can be used to give a very powerful push or as a strike.

In the application shown, it is used as a push. Assume that the elbow lock from the roll-back manoeuvre above has failed.

It would be a good idea to try to gain some distance from your opponent. Squeeze can be executed here for that purpose.

Press

1 The next application can flow on from the last one. If your squeeze was blocked with a rising block, as shown, you need to perform a follow-on technique.

2 When you feel that your movement has been redirected, you should separate your hands. As you pull your body back, you should allow your arms to retract. This will pull your opponent's blocking arm down.

3 When you are in the retracted position, mechanical energy is stored in your muscles like a compressed spring. You release the tension on the spring by pushing forward with your right heel and extending through your body. This will give you a very powerful two-handed push.

Single whip

The single-whip movement can look very impressive when performed in an explosive way. Both of your hands are used for striking attacks. The hands point in different directions, so your body should be centrally placed.

For the application shown, either the left or right hand could be used for an attack to the neck.

This demonstrates an attack with the right hand.

Here the left hand is sued to strike at the neck.

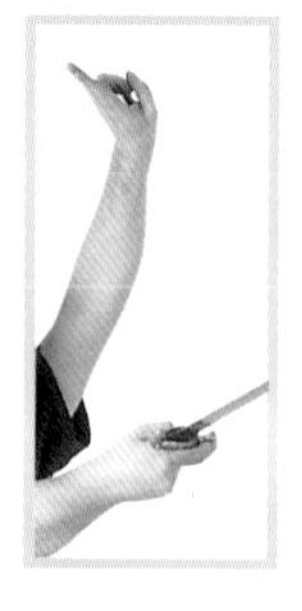

weapon forms

When a martial arts' student has reached a good level of skill with bare-hand forms, weapon forms are frequently studied. Forms such as the Tai Chi sword and sabre forms are dismissed by some as being out of date. The reasoning behind this is that nobody carries sword or sabres today.

This is a reasoning that has not thought deeply about the forms. For Tai Chi, as well as most other martial arts, the weapon and hand forms use similar, if not identical, techniques. If you can perform a technique properly with the bare-hand forms, you will have another challenge when it comes to a weapon technique. This will improve the depth of your understanding of the movement.

Precision is also an important factor in weapon training. If you practise your open-hand form with your hand-finishing slightly out of place, it can be difficult to notice. If you practise the same technique with a sword in your hand that is approximately 1 metre (3 feet) long, you errors will be amplified. This will make you automatically correct your technique.

After some time, the same level of accuracy will reflect itself within your bare-hand forms.

'Five-element palm' from the Tai Chi sabre form. The sword should remain firm and straight in your hand.

'Big dipper', from the Tai Chi sword form, shows poise and balance.

Your body alignment will be the same in weapon and open-hand forms.

index

a

b

c

d

e

f

g

h

i

j

k

l

m

n

o

p

q

r

s

Credits and acknowledgments

I would like to thank Carol for her help and support, all of my martial art teachers, especially Shelagh Grandpierre of the Tai Chi Alliance, Christopher Pei of the US Wushu Academy, Farhad of the Nottingham Trent University Tae Kwon Do team, and my brother, Mark, for his expert help with many aspects of the book.

The author and publishers would also like to thank the models:

Maria Costantino
Mark Pawlett, WTF Tae Kwon Do. 2nd Dan
Katy Woods
Grant Woolven, ITF Taekwondo. 1st Dan. Grant would particularly like to thank Mr Tan Eng Kiat, Vision Taekwondo, Malaysia, for his relentless and dedicated training.

With special thanks to Mr A Carter, A.B.A.P.T. ITF Taekwond-Do, of Denver, Downham Market, Norfolk, for supply of martial arts equipment.